Ships from SCOTLAND to North America 1830–1860

by
David Dobson

CLEARFIELD

Printed for
Clearfield Company, Inc. by
Genealogical Publishing Co., Inc.
Baltimore, Maryland
2002

International Standard Book Number: 0-8063-5151-9

Made in the United States of America

INTRODUCTION

During the eighteenth century, opportunities for emigration from Scotland were largely determined by the availability of shipping on the transatlantic trade routes. People might wait at ports for months or walk hundreds of miles in search of a ship. Exceptionally, occasional vessels would be specially chartered. The voyage of the <u>Hector</u> in 1773 was the first ship chartered to convey emigrants from the Highlands of Scotland to Canada.

Unlike modern transportation, in these early days of transatlantic shipping, vessels could and did sail from ports and bays all around the coastline. The early Victorian period was to witness great changes in the organization of emigration and transatlantic trade. Intermittent voyages of ships from Scotland to North America were to be replaced by a relatively integrated system whereby the railways would transport emigrants to major ports. The introduction at this period of steamships enabled regular timetables of departure from the west-coast ports of Greenock and Glasgow, and these provided a more reliable service and safer voyage. Growing demand for passage to Canada and the United States of America led to the introduction of vessels largely or wholly committed to passengers, although merchant vessels continued to transport emigrants also. By mid century, about half the passenger trade was by steamships, partly because of the increased capacity of these vessels.

Because the government of the United States imposed stricter regulations in the ratio of space to passengers and would not permit ships to dock which did not comply, emigrants took passage on British vessels bound for Canadian ports rather than American ones. This enabled the maintenance of cheaper passage, although emigrants had to endure extremely cramped conditions on board. On landing, a significant proportion of emigrants moved, as soon as possible, south to the United States.

The mid-nineteenth century was a period noted for the high level of emigration from Europe to North America. The reasons for this were varied but in the case of Scotland, the most important were the Highland Clearances and the Great Highland Famine. During the early nineteenth century vast tracts of Highland estates were cleared of their inhabitants by landowners, mostly clan chiefs, to provide land for large sheep farms. Those evicted from Highland areas were in most cases deposited on the coast and left to fate. Their choices were few. They had either to learn to fish and survive at subsistence level on coastal holdings, migrate south to the industrial Lowlands, or go abroad.

Some argue that there was a Malthusian situation existing, where the population of the Highlands was beginning to exceed the land's ability to feed them, and that famine or emigration were likely outcomes. The communities of the north-west Highlands and Islands were, like much of Ireland, too reliant on the potato, and its failure and the subsequent famine was a major cause of emigration.

Although the emigration of Highlanders was significant, there were also other groups crossing the Atlantic in search of a better life. The continuing agricultural revolution, which caused mergers of small farms into more efficient units, and the improvements in agricultural practices resulted in a surplus of farm workers. Similarly, improvements in industrial technology, such as in the textile industry, resulted in labour surpluses. Skilled industrial and professional workers began to see the opportunities offered in the New World. All these factors were at play during the period, impacting on transatlantic shipping.

Without claiming to be definitive, this book lists the majority of vessels leaving Scotland for North America between 1830 and 1860. The predominant source used was contemporary Scottish newspapers, in which reference is made to voyages. Unfortunately, the information they provide on passengers is vague, some noting the number of passengers carried and others simply that they are carrying passengers. However, the book includes all vessels found to be sailing to North America at this period in the knowledge that all would have been able to take passengers, and it is known that vessels often casually picked up emigrants en-route.

This book is designed as an aid to researchers, to enable them to link the place that their immigrant ancestors were first recorded in North America with their port of embarkation in Scotland and thus possibly the region of origin of the emigrant.

David Dobson
St Andrews, Scotland, 2002

SHIPS FROM SCOTLAND
TO NORTH AMERICA, 1830-1860

A. AND J. FULTON, Captain Lovett, arrived in Boston 10 January
1861 from Ardrossan. [S#1749]

ABOELLINO, an American ship, from the Clyde to New York in June
1854. [EEC#22609]

ABEONA, Captain Shields, arrived in Montreal on 27 May 1850 from
Arbroath; from Arbroath to Quebec and Montreal on 29 July
1850. [EEC#21978/22000]

ABERDEEN, 560 tons, Captain Duffy, from Glasgow *with*
passengers to Quebec and Montreal in April 1843. [GSP#779]

ABERDEENSHIRE, a brig, from Aberdeen *with 20 passengers*
bound for Nova Scotia, landed at Halifax in September 1831,
[AR:3.9.1831]; from Aberdeen *with 40 passengers* bound
for Nova Scotia, landed at Halifax in April 1832,
[TN:26.4.1832];from Aberdeen *with 39 passengers* bound
for Nova Scotia, landed at Halifax in September 1832,
[TN:20.9.1832]; from Aberdeen *with 13 passengers* bound
for Nova Scotia, arrived in Halifax on 13 April 1833,
[PANS#282/81]; from Aberdeen from Aberdeen *with 24*
passengers bound for Halifax, Pictou and Miramachi in 1834,
arrived in Halifax in May 1834. [Abdn.Herald,18.1.1834]
[TN:8.5.1834]; Captain Martin, from Aberdeen on 5 August
1834 *with 11 passengers* bound for Halifax, Pictou and
Miramachi, arrived in Halifax in September 1834. [AJ#4517]
[TN:18.9.1834] ; a 422 ton barque. Captain Alexander Smith,
from Aberdeen *with passengers* bound for Quebec on 2 June
1837. [AJ#4664]

ABIGAIL, 632 tons, Captain Daly, from the Broomielaw, Glasgow,
with 360 passengers bound for Quebec and Montreal on 5
June 1844. [GSP#855/860]

ACADIA, a barque, from Greenock *with 9 passengers* bound for
Nova Scotia, landed at Halifax in October 1832,
[AR:6.10.1832]; from Greenock *with 8 passengers* bound for
Nova Scotia, landed at Halifax on 19 April 1833; from Greenock
on 8 September 1833 *with 11 passengers* bound for Nova
Scotia, landed at Halifax on 11 October 1833. [PANS#282/81];
Captain Hamilton Auld, from Greenock *with passengers*
bound for Halifax, Nova Scotia, on 25 August 1834.
[SG#3/270]

ACADIA OF LEITH, bound for Quebec in May 1842. [EEC#20373];
364 tons, Captain Younger, from Glasgow *with passengers*

bound for Quebec and Montreal on 2 April 1844; from the
Clyde to Yarmouth, Nova Scotia, in December 1847; from
Montrose to Quebec on 12 April 1849.
[GSP#848][EEC#21039/21619/21798]

ACADIAN, a 387 ton barque, Captain Hamilton Auld, from Greenock
on 2 April 1834 *with 14 passengers* bound for Nova Scotia,
arrived at Halifax by 1 May 1834. [SG#2/222] [TN:1.5.1834];
Captain Hamilton Auld, from Greenock *with 5 passengers*
bound for Halifax, Nova Scotia, and Charleston, South Carolina,
on 22 March 1839; from Greenock *with passengers* bound
for Halifax, Nova Scotia, and Charleston, South Carolina, on 20
August 1839. [SG#8/745, 786]; Captain F. Ritchie, from
Glasgow *with passengers* bound for Halifax, Nova Scotia, on
26 August 1845. [SG#14/1426]

ACADIAN, Captain Ritchie, from Glasgow to Halifax, shored on
Whitehead on 19 May 1847. [EEC#21514][AJ#5189]

ACADIAN, Captain Gardner, from the Clyde to Boston on 5 August
1849, [EEC#21846]

ACME, Captain Somerville, from the Clyde to Quebec on 4 April 1851;
from the Clyde to Quebec on 26 July 1851,
[EEC#22105/22153]

ACTEON OF GLASGOW, from the Clyde to Quebec in August 1855;
Captain Benson, from Greenock to New Orleans January 1861.
[EEC#322795][S#1737]

ACTIVE OF GREENOCK, bound for Richibucto in April 1844.
[EEC#21063]

ACTON, from Glasgow to New York in April 1847. [EEC#2148]

ACTRESS, Captain Flint, from the Clyde to Boston on 4 March 1851,
arrived in Boston on 17 April 1851. [EEC#22091/22117]

ADAM CARR OF GREENOCK, a 345 ton barque, from Glasgow to
Canada *with 131 passengers* on 1 May 1844, [BPP.35.503];
Captain McEwan, from Greenock to New York on 7 August
1845, [SG#14/1427]; Captain Wright, from the Clyde to New
York on 18 January 1847; from the Clyde to New York on 4
May 1847; Captain Craig, from the Clyde to New York on 16
May 1848; from the Clyde to New York on 8 April 1849; from
Glasgow to New York in July 1849; Captain White, from the
Clyde to New York on 16 March 1850; from Glasgow *with 32
passengers* bound for New York on 20 July 1850, arrived
there on 2 September 1850; from the Clyde to New York on 29
November 1850; from the Clyde to New York on 3 May 1851.
[EEC#21451/21497/21658/21795/ 21841/21942 /21995/22051
/22117] [USNA][SG#18/1832] [PC#1977]

ADELAIDE, from the Clyde to Boston in September 1849.
[EEC#21872]

ADELINE, Captain Cann, from the Clyde to Boston in August 1850.
[EEC#22013]

ADEPT, Captain Burns, from the Clyde to Quebec on 28 July 1849;
from the Clyde to Mobile on 14 November 1850; from the
Clyde to Mobile on 25 January 1853; from the Clyde to Quebec
in October 1853. [EEC#21843/22043/22387/22508]

ADIRONDACK, 700 tons, Captain Hackstaff, from Glasgow to New
York on 7 April 1841; from Glasgow *with passengers* bound
for New York on 8 October 1842. [GSP#659/773]

ADLER, Captain Hohurst, from the Clyde to New York on 7 April
1850. [EEC#21951]

ADMIRAL, Captain Crisp, from the Clyde to St John, New Brunswick,
on 17 August 1850, [EEC#22007]; from Lochboisdale and
Stornaway *with 413 (450) passengers from Barra and
South Uist* bound for Canada on 11 August 1851. [GHF#326][
Book of Barra#223][TGSI#55.342][Outer Isles,#136]

ADONIS, Captain McMillan, from the Clyde to Mobile on 15 October
1849; from the Clyde to New York on 30 March 1851.
[EEC#21876/22102]

ADVICE OF GLASGOW, from Glasgow to Quebec in September
1855. [EEC#322796]

AERIAL, a 286 ton brig, Captain Ritchie, from Dundee on 2 April
1846 *with 2 passengers* bound for Quebec, arrived there on
15 May 1846, [MG]; Captain Summersen, from Leith to Quebec
on 6 May 1853, [EEC#22429][LCL#4194]

AFGHAN, a 800 ton American bark, Captain Black, arrived in Quebec
on 12 May 1846 *with 4 passengers* from Greenock, [MT];
Captain E. Banzett, from Glasgow *with passengers* bound for
New York on 15 June 1847. [AJ#5185]; Captain Copland, from
the Clyde to New York on 5 April 1849; Captain Black, from the
Clyde to Quebec on 26 August 1850. [EEC#21793/22010]

AGAMEMNON, from the Clyde to Quebec in May 1853. [EEC#22448]

AGENORA, 920 tons, Captain McCulloch, from Aberdeen to
Charleston on 10 August 1837, [AJ#4675]; from Glasgow to
Quebec on 24 July 1841. [GSP#673]

AGITATOR, 400 tons, Captain Henry, from Glasgow to Quebec in
July 1840; from Glasgow to New York on 8 March 1841.
[GSP#655/681]

AGNES, a 450 ton brig, master Andrew Malcolm, from Leith *with 70
passengers* bound for New York on 25 March 1833.
[FJ#4][LCL#2095]

AGNES, Captain Outerbridge, from the Clyde to Quebec in 1833.
[SG#2/170]

AGNES AND ANN, Captain Anderson, from the Clyde to Quebec on
15 August 1849. [EEC#21850]

AGNES GILMOUR OF GLASGOW, bound for Quebec in June 1843.
[EEC#20628]

AGNES PRIMROSE, 165 ton brig, master Andrew Johnston, from Glasgow *with passengers* to Montreal in April 1832.
[GkAd#3827]

AGNES SOPHIA, Captain Bett, from the Clyde to Boston on 29 April 1850; from the Clyde to Pictou on 7 April 1851.
[EEC#21960/22105]

AGNEDA, Captain Fell, from the Clyde to Quebec on 24 July 1845.
[SG#14/1423]

AIM, Captain Gibson, arrived at St John, Newfoundland, on 15 May 1850 from the Clyde; from the Clyde to the Columbia River on 18 July 1851. [EEC#21978/22149]

AIMWELL, Captain Morrison, from Aberdeen *with passengers* bound for Quebec in 1832. [AJ.7.3.1832]

ALABAMA, 680 tons, Captain Percy, from Glasgow *with passengers* bound for New York on 31 August 1840.
[GSP#690]

ALARM, 330 tons, Captain Brown, from Glasgow *with passengers* to Quebec and Montreal on 1 May 1841. [GSP#662]

ALASCO, 449 tons, Captain John Lombard, from Glasgow *with passengers* bound for New York on 17 July 1841.
[GSP#668/673]

ALBERT, 305 tons, from Greenock *with passengers* bound for St John, New Brunswick, in May 1841, arrived there on 5 July 1841. [GSP#662]

ALBERT, 513 tons, from Glasgow to Philadelphia on 7 October 1841. [GSP#683]

ALBERT, a barque, Captain Card, from Glasgow *with passengers* bound for Boston on 27 January 1848. [SG#17/1684]

ALBERT, Captain Hayler, from Troon to Montreal on 13 April 1848; Captain Smart, from Aberdeen to Quebec on 12 April 1849; from Aberdeen to Quebec on 11 April 1850; from Aberdeen to Quebec on 16 April 1851, arrived there on 26 May 1851.
[EEC#21645/21797/21955/22110] [LCL#3977][AJ#5397]

ALBION, from Greenock *with 191 passengers, mainly Highlanders* bound for Quebec and Upper Canada on 2 June 1829, [EEC#18339]; from Tobermory, Mull, *with 59 passengers* bound for Nova Scotia, landed at Sydney, Cape Breton Island, on 5 August 1832, [PANS#282/48]; from Glasgow *with 90 passengers* bound for Montreal in April 1833. [Times#15146]; arrived at St Ann's, Nova Scotia, on 6 December 1836 *with 75 passengers* from Tobermory, Mull. [PANS#252/101]

ALBION, 471 tons, from Glasgow to Quebec on 5 April 1841; from Glasgow to Montreal in March 1845; Captain Bryce Allan, from the Clyde to Montreal on 15 July 1845, [SG#14/1420]; from Greenock to Quebec on 25 March 1847, arrived there on 4 June 1847; Captain McArthur, from the Clyde to Montreal on 27 March 1849; from the Clyde to Montreal on 19 July 1849; from Greenock to Montreal on 16 July 1850. [EEC#21159/21790/21838/21995][GSP#659]

ALBION OF ABERDEEN, a 266 ton brig, Captain Alexander Leslie, arrived at Halifax *with 17 passengers* from Aberdeen on 23 April 1831, [AR:23.4.1831]; from Aberdeen *with 31 passengers* bound for Nova Scotia, landed at Halifax in April 1831, [TN:19.4.1832]; from Aberdeen *with 26 passengers* bound for Nova Scotia, landed at Halifax on 13 April 1833, [PANS#282/81]; from Aberdeen on 15 August 1833 *with 21 passengers* bound for Nova Scotia, landed at Halifax on 16 September 1833, [PANS#282/81]; from Aberdeen on 25 July 1834 *with 37 passengers* bound for Halifax, Pictou and Miramachi, arrived there in September 1834, [AJ#4516][TN:18.9.1834]; from Aberdeen *with passengers* bound for Halifax, Nova Scotia, *"only two days sailing from the United States"*, in 1835. [AJ,21.1.1835]; arrived in Halifax in May 1836 *with 38 passengers* from Aberdeen, [TN:12.5.1836];from Aberdeen *with passengers* bound for Halifax and Miramachi on 25 July 1836, [AJ#4620]; arrived in Halifax in September 1836 *with 49 passengers* from Aberdeen, [TN:22.9.1836]; from Aberdeen *with 15 passengers* bound for Nova Scotia on 27 March 1837, arrived in Halifax in April 1837, [AJ#4654][AR:29.4.1837]; from Aberdeen *with passengers* bound for Miramachi on 5 August 1837, [AJ#4673]; arrived at Halifax in September 1837 *with 26 passengers* from Aberdeen, [AR:9.9.1837]; from Aberdeen *with 21 passengers* bound for Halifax and Miramachi on 1 August 1838, [AJ#4725]; arrived in Halifax in September 1838, [TN:6.9.1838]; from Aberdeen *with passengers* bound for Halifax and Miramachi on 16 March 1839; from Aberdeen *with 30 passengers* to Halifax and Miramachi on 5 August 1839; from Aberdeen to Halifax on 25 March 1840; from Aberdeen *with passengers* bound for Halifax and Miramachi on 27 July 1840, arrived in Miramachi on 19 September 1840 from Aberdeen, [AJ#4750/4779/4812/4828/4842]; from Aberdeen to Halifax, Nova Scotia, in August 1843. [EEC#20648] [DW#128]; Captain Alexander Leslie, from Aberdeen *with passengers* bound for Halifax, and St John's, New Brunswick, on 10 March 1846, *"passengers going to the United States will find Halifax a favourable port to disembark at, there being regular steamers from thence running to the States".* [AJ#5118]; from Aberdeen to Halifax and St Johns, NB, *with passengers* on 4 March 1847, [AJ#5167]; from Aberdeen *with passengers* bound for Halifax, Nova Scotia, in 1847, [CNSHS#23.46]; from Aberdeen to St John's, New Brunswick, on 14 March 1849; from Aberdeen to Halifax on 6 August 1849; from Aberdeen to St John, New Brunswick, 5 April 1850; from Aberdeen *with passengers* bound to Halifax on 2 April 1851; from Aberdeen *with pasengers* bound for Halifax, Nova Scotia, 4 August 1851; from Aberden to Halifax 15 April 1853. [AJ#5377/5402][LCL#3872/4188] [EEC#21784/21847/22104]

ALCESTE, Captain Manson, from the Clyde to Montreal on 3 September 1850. [EEC#22014]

ALDEBARAN, from the Clyde to Quebec on 1 August 1849. [EEC#21844/21855]

ALDERMAN THOMSON, Captain Anderson, arrived in Quebec in July 1840 from Wick. [AJ#4828]

ALERT, Captain Hogg, arrived in Quebec on 6 July 1834 from Peterhead. [AJ#4515]

ALESTO, 470 tons, Captain Whiting, from Glasgow to New Orleans in March 1841, [GSP#655]

ALEXANDER, Captain Carmichael, from Greenock to New York on 6 January 1832. [GkAd#3804]

ALEXANDER, a 315 ton barque, Captain Primrose, from Leith *with passengers* bound for Quebec and Montreal on 1 April 1842. [EEC#20338]

ALEXANDER, Captain Jack, from the Clyde to Boston on 6 July 1850. [EEC#21990]

ALEXANDER BROWN, from the Clyde to Boston in August 1849. [EEC#21855]

ALEXANDER HALL, Captain Morrison, from Aberdeen to Quebec on 30 April 1851, arrived there on 11 June 1851. [EEC#22116][AJ#5399]

ALEXANDER HARVEY, Captain Rosie, from Aberdeen to Quebec on 30 July 1849, [EEC#21844]

ALEYONE, Captain Watson, from the Clyde to Boston on 4 March 1850. [EEC#21936]

ALFRED, Captain Thomson, from Leith *with 1 passenger* bound for New Brunswick in September 1832; from Leith *with 240 passengers* bound for Quebec on 23 May 1834, arrived in Quebec on 7 July 1834. [LCL#2039][FJ#73][MG]

ALFRED, a 450 ton American ship, from leith *with 234 passengers* to Quebec 15 May 1834, [LCL#2214]; Captain J. C. Myers, from Glasgow *with passengers* bound for New York on 26 June 1844. [GSP#860]

ALFRED, a barque, Captain Ford, from Leith to St John's, New Brunswick, on 10 March 1849; from Leith to Quebec in August 1850. [EEC#21783/22023]

ALFRED, 342 tons, Captain White, from Alloa to Miramachi 1 April 1840, [LCL]; Captain Beveridge, from Alloa to St Johns on 23 May 1841, [LCL#3468]; from Alloa to Canada *with 1 passengers* on 3 April 1843; from Alloa to Canada *with 1 passenger* on 19 March 1844, [BPP.35.503]; Captain Graham, from Leith to Quebec 3 April 1850; from Leith to St John on 2 April 1851. [LCL#3870/3974]

ALHAMBRA, 715 tons, Captain Wilson, from Glasgow *with passengers* bound for New Orleans on 6 August 1841. [GSP#676]

ALLAN OF GLASGOW, to Quebec in June 1850. [EEC#21980]

ALLAN, Captain McArthur, from the Clyde to Quebec 14 April 1858. [CM#21393]

ALLAN BROWN, Captain Shaw, from the Clyde to Boston on16 June 1849, [EEC#21825]

ALLAN KERR, *with 18 passengers* bound for Canada in 1853. [BPP.46.31]

ALLEGHANY, a 530 ton American ship, from Glasgow to Philadelphia on 1 September 1840; Captain Ames, from Glasgow *with passengers* bound for Philadelphia on 25 March 1843. [GSP#690/779]

ALMA, Captain Frizle, from Greenock to Boston in April 1855. [EEC#22722]

ALMIRA, 460 tons, Captain Weeks, from Glasgow to New York on 9 May 1840. [GSP#673]

ALTONA, Captain Leslie, from Aberdeen to St John, New Brunswick, on 16 August 1850. [EEC#22007]

AMANDA, a brig, Captain Anderson, from Leith to Montreal on 1 April 1841. [EEC#20168]

AMAZON, a brig, Captain Philip Blues, from Leith *with 2 passengers* bound for Richmond, Virginia, in June 1831. [EEC#18648][LCL#19/1909]

AMBASSADOR, a 452 ton American ship, Captain Cornelius Meany, from Glasgow *with passengers* bound for New York on 10 July 1842. [GSP#724]

AMELIA, Captain Cann, from the Clyde to Boston on 1 March 1851, arrived in Boston on 8 April 1851; from the Clyde to Boston on 26 February 1853. [EEC#22090/22114/22401]

AMELIA HILL, Captain Hill, from the Clyde to Montreal on 6 July 1850. [EEC#21990]

AMELIA STRONG, a 320 ton American ship, Captain Pelham, from Glasgow *with passengers* bound for Boston on 3 August 1840. [GSP#685]

AMERICA, a 620 ton American ship, Captain Ansell L. Dyer, from Glasgow *with passengers* bound for New York on 30 May 1840; from Glasgow *with passengers* bound for New York on 15 September 1841; from Glasgow *with passengers* bound for New York on 31 May 1842; Captain Waite, from Glasgow *with passengers* bound for New York on 7 April 1843 and on 7 August 1843. [GSP#676/682/716/791]; Captain Stephenson, arrived in Boston on 11 April 1851 from the Clyde; Captain Beckwith, from the Clyde to New York on 26 February 1853. [EEC#22114/22401]

AMERICA OF ST ANN'S, NOVA SCOTIA, from the Clyde to New York in August 1853. [EEC#22481]

AMERICAN, Captain Guthrie, from the Clyde to Montreal on 29 March 1851. [EEC#22102]

AMERICAN LASS OF GLASGOW, 764 tons, Captain John McKellar, from Greenock *with 280 passengers* bound for New York on 10 June 1851, ship returned to port storm damaged on 18 June 1851; Captain Carmichael, from the Clyde to New York on 27 June 1851 [EEC#22136/22141]

AMITH, arrived in Prince Edward Island during 1832 from Glasgow. [TIM#17.36]

AMITY, a brig, from Tobermory, Mull, *with 258 passengers* bound for Cape Breton Island, in 1833, landed at Ship Harbour, Nova Scotia, on 21 August 1833. [CNSHS#23.46][PANS/Financial Mss, Passenger Money]

AMITY, a brig, Captain Mercer, from Greenock on 24 May 1834 *with 35 passengers* bound for Quebec, arrived there on 6 July 1834. [MG]

AMITY OF ABERDEEN, a 311 ton brig, Captain David M. Rae, from Aberdeen to Quebec 1835/1836. [FAO#79]; arrived in Quebec on 3 June 1836 from Aberdeen; Captain Leslie, from Aberdeen to Quebec on 14 April 1838; Captain Cumming, from Aberdeen to the Bay of Chaleur on 13 April 1839; Captain John Dempster, from Aberdeen *with 3 passengers* bound for Dalhousie in April 1840; arrived in Dalhousie on 9 September 1840 from Aberdeen. [AJ#4619/4711/4760/4815/4841]

AMITY OF GLASGOW, possibly from Mull, Argyll, *with passengers* bound for Prince Edward Island, arrived there on 11 August 1853. [PAPEI: MG24.I.10]

ANDREW WHITE, a 256 ton brig, Captain Benjamin Clarke, from Glasgow *with passengers* bound for Montreal on 15 June 1841. [GSP#667]

ANDROMEDA, Captain Peat, from Dundee to Quebec on 27 March 1850; from Dundee to Quebec on 21 August 1850; Captain Foote, from Dundee to Quebec on 2 April 1851. [EEC#21948/22009/22104]

ANGLESEA, Captain Crawford, from the Clyde to Quebec in May 1858, [CM#21419]

ANGLO SAXON, from Glasgow via Londonderry *with passengers* to Portland 8 March 1861. [S#1757]

ANN, Captain Mason, from Leith to Liverpool, Nova Scotia, on 13 July 1829, [LCL#1710]; from Leith to Miramachi on 14 April 1830, [LCL#1788]

ANN, 300 tons, Captain George Rodgers, from Leith *with 51 passengers* bound for Quebec and Montreal on 28 June 1832. [CM#17304][LCL#2019]; Captain Wallace, from Leith *with 25 passengers* bound for Montreal in April 1838. [LCL#2624]

ANNE, a brig, Captain Blair, from Dumfries on 22 May 1834 *with 180 passengers* bound for Quebec, arrived there on 7 July 1834. [MG]

ANNE, Captain Miller, arrived in St John's, New Brunswick, on 25 April 1850 from Kirkcudbright, [EEC#21966]; Captain Banks, from Kirkcudbright to Quebec 14 April 1858, [CM#21391]

ANN CLAPERTON, 417 tons, Captain John Claperton, from Greenock *with passengers* bound for New York on 5 June 1834. [SG#3/250]

ANN DUNN, from the Clyde to Newfoundland on 7 September 1849. [EEC#21861]

ANN ELIZABETH, from Leith to Prince Edward Island, arrived there on 23 June 1846. [PAPEI]

ANN GRANT, from Greenock *with 11 passengers* bound for Nova Scotia, arrived in Pictou on 16 June 1836; from Greenock *with 11 passengers* bound for Nova Scotia, arrived at Pictou on 29 September 1836. [PANS#252/90]; from the Clyde to Quebec in May 1840. [EEC#20058]

ANN HARLEY, a 454 ton barque, Captain Robert Scott, from Glasgow bound for New York *with 43 passengers*, arrived in New York in December 1846, [USNA/par]; from Glasgow *with passengers* to New York on 2 July 1847. [EEC#21523]; from Glasgow to New York on 28 July 1848, [SG#17/1736]; from Glasgow *with 15 passengers* bound for New York, arrived there on 29 May 1849. [USNA]; from Glasgow *with passengers* to New York on 21 August 1849; Captain Craig, from the Clyde to New York on 10 October 1850; from the

Clyde to New York on 6 March 1851; Captain Logan, from the Clyde to New York on 18 July 1851; from Glasgow *with 41 passengers* on 15 August 1851. [BPP#68] [EEC#21852/22029/22093/22149][SG#18/1847]

ANN HENZELL, a 278 ton snow, master Thomas S. Henzell, from Glasgow to Quebec and Montreal *with 75 passengers* on 25 April 1844; from Glasgow to Montreal on 11 May 1844. [GSP#854][BPP.35.503]

ANN JOHNSTON, Captain Corbin, from Greenock *with 2 passengers* bound for Newfoundland on 31 July 1839, [SG#8/791]; Captain Soper, from the Clyde to Newfoundland on 7 April 1849; from the Clyde to Newfoundland on 4 September 1849; Captain Cleary, from the Clyde to Newfoundland on 12 August 1850. [EEC#21795/21859/22005]

ANN MARTIN, Captain Roubuck, from Greenock to New Orleans via Jamaica on 17 September 1839, [SG#8/804]

ANN RANKIN, Captain Green, from the Clyde to Bathurst on 13 July 1850; Captain Burns, from the Clyde to Montreal on 2 May 1851. [EEC#21993/22117]; from Glasgow *with 22 passengers* on 22 June 1851, [BPP#68]

ANNA, Captain Rees, from the Clyde to New York on 26 June 1851, [EEC#22140]

ANNA JENKINS, Captain Lloyd, from the Clyde to San Francisco on 27 March 1853. [EEC#22401]

ANNA MARY, 213 tons, from Banff and Fraserburgh to Canada *with 29 passengers* on 15 April 1843; from Banff to Canada *with 2 passengers* on 2 August 1843. [BPP.35.503]

ANNANDALE, a 256 ton brig, Captain Craig, from Aberdeen *with passengers* bound for Quebec on 1 April 1837; from Aberdeen *with passengers* bound for Quebec on 12 August 1837; from Aberdeen *with passengers* bound for Quebec on 10 April 1839; from Aberdeen to Quebec on 1 August 1838; from Aberdeen *with passengers* bound for Quebec on 16 August 1839; Captain Lewis, from the clyde to Quebec 8 June 1858 [AJ#4651/4674/4726/4759/4780][CM#21438]

ANNETTE, from Dundee to America in May 1841. [EEC#20219]

ANNIE, Captain Rees, from the Clyde to New York on 28 June 1851, [EEC#22141]

ANNIE HALL, Captain Filson, arrived in New York on 28 December 1860 from Ardrossan. [S#1737]

ANO, 483 tons, from Glasgow to New York on 26 February 1842 *"the railroad now open from Boston to Buffalo renders the route by Boston the most expeditious and cheap mode of travel to Upper Canada, New Brunswick and the Western States".* [GSP#702][GH#4071]

ANT, Captain Williams, from the Clyde to St John's, New Brunswick, on 10 March 1849; from the Clyde to St John, New Brunswick, on 5 March 1850, arrived there on 25 April 1850. [EEC#21783/21937/21966]

APOLLO, a 276 ton barque, Captain Henry Walker, arrived in Quebec on 29 June 1837 from Dundee. [AJ#4674]; from Dundee to Canada *with 11 passengers* on 20 August 1842; from Dundee to Canada *with 42 passengers* on 3 April 1843, [DW#107]; from Dundee to Canada *with 26 passengers* on 17 August 1843, [DW#126]; from Dundee to Montreal *with 48 passengers* on 3 April 1844, [BPP.35.503][DW#157]; from Dundee to Montreal *with passengers* in August 1844, [DW#181]; from Dundee to Montreal *with passengers* in April 1845, [DW#209]; from Dundee *with passengers* bound for Quebec and Montreal on 15 August 1845, [NW#5/235]; from Dundee *with 54 passengers* bound for Montreal on 28 March 1846, arrived there on 21 May 1846, [DPCA#2331][QG][MT]

ARAB, Captain Stott, from Aberdeen to Quebec on 12 April 1850, arrived there on 15 May 1850 [EEC#21955/21976][LCL#875]

ARABIAN, 371 tons, Captain Allan, from Glasgow to Montreal in July 1838; Captain Auld, from Glasgow *with 14 passengers* bound for Montreal on 26 March 1839; from Greenock to Montreal on 24 August 1839, [SG#7/681; 8/756; 8/798]; Captain Greenhorn, from Glasgow *with passengers* to Montreal, wrecked in Griffins Cove, Gaspe Bay, on 1 April 1840, *all 8 passengers saved.* [EEC#20064][AJ#4823]

ARABIAN, 450 tons, Captain Shaw, from Glasgow *with passengers* bound for Quebec on 10 May 1843. [GSP#800]; Captain McKenzie, from the Clyde to New York on 27 March 1853. [EEC#22401]; Captain Shaw, from the Clyde to Halifax, NS, 9 April 1858. [CM#21388]

ARAMINTA, from Glasgow *with passengers* bound for Quebec on 1 June 1843. [DW#121]

ARCADIAN, Captain Gardner, from the Clyde to Boston on 2 August 1849, [EEC#21845]

ARDGOWAN OF WIGTOWN, a brig, from Garlieston on 13 April 1842, wrecked at sea on 6 May 1842. [EEC#20390]

ARENDAL, Captain Jorgensen, from Leith to Quebec 19 April 1854. [LCL#4293]

ARGENTIUS, a 540 ton barque, Captain Currie, from Leith *with passengers* bound for Quebec in April 1854. [EEC#22549]

ARGO OF PRUSSIA, a 500 ton barque, Captain Alexander Breslack, from Leith *with passengers* bound for Quebec on 8 June 1850, via Thurso *with 59 passengers from Lochinver,*

West Sutherland bound for Canada in June 1850; from the Clyde to Philadelphia on 18 June 1851, [GHF#324][I A, 25.6.1850] [EEC#21970/21977/22136] [LCL#3889]

ARGO, Captain Mitchell, from the Clyde to Quebec on 8 August 1850; from the Clyde to Mobile on 6 December 1850. [EEC#22002/22053]

ARGUS, Captain Harrison, from Leith to Miramachi on 20 April 1853, [EEC#22422]

ARGYLE, Captain Fletcher, from the Clyde to Savannah on 24 October 1850; from the Clyde to New York in August 1853; from the Clyde to New York, wrecked on Squam Beach on 28 January 1855, "*1 passenger drowned*". [EEC#22036/22483/22699]

ARIEL, a 200 ton brig, Captain David Ritchie, from Dundee *with 2 passengers* bound for Montreal in March 1846, arrived in Quebec on 15 May 1846, [DPCA#2319][MT]; from Leith to Quebec and Montreal on 5 April 1847. [EEC#21474]

ARK, a 296 ton American brig, Captain Samuel Flanders, from Glasgow *with passengers* bound for New York on 2 October 1839. [SG#8/801]

ARKWRIGHT, Captain James Birnie, arrived in New York from Dundee on 31 October 1831 *with 8 passengers*, [USNA#ms237/15]; from Dundee to New York, arrived there on 13 September 1833. [FH#602]; from Aberdeen *with passengers* bound for New York on 29 August 1834, arrived in New York on 8 October 1834. [AJ#4515/4521/4531]; from Aberdeen *with 164 passengers* bound for New York on 25 April 1837. [AJ#4646/4659]

ARRAGON, 741 tons, Captain Knight, from Glasgow *with passengers* bound for New York on 26 July 1844. [GSP#861/866]

ARRAN OF GLASGOW, from the Clyde to Quebec in May 1853; from Glasgow to Quebec in August 1854; Captain Higgins, arrived in New orleans 4 January 1861 from the Clyde. [EEC#22444/22633][S#1752]

ASHLEY, from the Clyde to St Johns in August 1854. [EEC#22636]

ASIA, 550 tons, Captain Sears, from Glasgow to New Orleans in January 1841; Captain Hannay, from Glasgow *with passengers* bound for Quebec and Montreal on 1 April 1843. [GSP#647/779]; Captain Chalmers, from the Clyde to Newfoundland on 26 July 1845, [SG#14/1424]

ASPHALON, Captain Gordon, from Stromness to Quebec 26 April 1858, [CM#21406]

ATALANTA, 406 tons, Captain Raymond, from Glasgow *with passengers* bound for New York on 23 June 1844.
[GSP#861]
ATHAL, Captain Currie, from the Clyde to New Richmond on 31 July 1845, [SG#14/1422]
ATHENS, 600 tons, Captain Chase, from Glasgow *with passengers* bound for New York on 12 June 1842.
[GSP#719]
ATHOLL, Captain Duthie, from Dundee to New York on 4 January 1831. [PA#75]
ATHOLL, Captain McCready, from Greenock to St John, New Brunswick, wrecked near Barrington, Nova Scotia, on 30 June 1835. [FJ#137]
ATLANTIC, Captain Hardenbrook, from Greenock to St John, New Brunswick, on 20 September 1838; from Glasgow to St John, New Brunswick, on 28 March 1839. [SG#7/702; 8/755]
ATLANTIC OF PERTH, a 284 ton barque, Captain George Morton, from Dundee *with 27 passengers* bound for Quebec, 8 April 1840, [LCL]; wrecked on Cape St Francis, Newfoundland, on 5 May 1840. [AJ#4822][EEC#20062]
ATLANTIC OF PERTH, a 300 ton barque, Capt. Morton, *with passengers* was wrecked off Cape Francois on 5 May 1860. [EEC#20062]
ATLANTIC, 672 tons, Captain Mallet, from Glasgow *with passengers* bound for New Orleans on 25 August 1844.[GSP#867]
ATLANTIC, *with 209 passengers from Barra and South Uist* bound for Canada in 1849. [GHF#325] [TGSI#55.342]
ATLANTIC OF LIVERPOOL, 1042 tons, Captain Ross, from Ardrossan *with 300 passengers from Knapdale and 200 from Uist* bound for Montreal on 14 July 1849. [EEC#21838][SG#18/1824, 1834]
ATLAS, Captain Nicholls, arrived in New York on 18 June 1834 from Dundee. [AJ#4514]
AUCKLAND, 400 tons, Captain Atkins, from Glasgow *with passengers* bound for Montreal on 17 July 1842. [GSP#724]
AUGUST ADOLPH, Captain Hohn, from Montrose to New York on 24 May 1849. [EEC#21817]
AUGUSTA, Captain Crowe, from the Clyde to New York on 17 May 1848; from the Clyde to New York on 28 March 1849. [EEC#21658/21790]
AURORA, master Alexander Morrison, from Aberdeen *with 150 passengers* bound for America in April 1854; arrived in Quebec on 21 May 1854; from Aberdeen on 19 April 1855

with 338 passengers bound for Quebec.
[SRO.CE87.1.30][Neil MS, Aberdeen Public Library] [AJ#5562]
AVALANCHE, Captain Hawkins, from the Clyde to New York on 4
    September 1850. [EEC#22014]
AVALON, Captain Ritchie, from Greenock to Newfoundland on 2 July
    1838; from Greenock to Newfoundland on 23 July 1839.
    [SG#7/679; 8/789]
BALCLUTHA, Captain Hart, from the Clyde to Newfoundland on 22
    July 1850. [EEC#21997]
BARLOW, 436 tons, Captain Fell, from Greenock **with 90
    passengers** bound for New York on 23 February 1842,
    **"times of sailing have been chosen to enable emigrants
    to reach their destination at the beginning of the
    season when wages are at their highest and rates of
    passage half the usual later in the
    season.**[EEC#20333][GSP#700] [GH#4071] ;Captain Fraser,
    from the Clyde **with 263 passengers from Mull** bound for
    Quebec and Montreal on 28 June 1849.[Argyll Estate
    Papers#1535, Inveraray Castle][EEC#21829]; from Sutherland
    via Stornaway **with 287 passengers** bound for Canada on 21
    June 1851. [GHF#220/325/326] [TGSI#55.340]
BARCILIEU, arrived in Newfoundland from the Clyde in 1849.
    [SG#18/1835]
BARONET, 350 tons, Captain J. Rankine, from Leith **with 59
    passengers** bound for Quebec on 9 June 1831.
    [EEC#18648][LCL#1908]
BAROSSA, 252 tons, Captain Duncanson, from Leith to Montreal in
    April 1854. [LCL#4291]
BEATRICE, Captain Pryde, from Dundee to New York on 17 June
    1830. [PA#46]
BEAVER, 450 tons, Captain John Edmonds, from Glasgow **with
    passengers** bound for Boston on 15 September 1841.
    **"emigrants at this season of the year proceeding to
    Upper and Lower Canada, the Northern and Western
    States, Prince Edward Island, Halifax and Pictou will
    find Boston by far the most expeditious and cheap
    rate."** [GSP#681]; from Ardrossan to New York, arrived at
    Yarmouth, Nova Scotia, on 9 February 1860. [DC#23477]
BELLISARIUS, an American brigantine, Captain James Tibbets, from
    Greenock **with passengers** bound for Boston on 28 July
    1802. [CM#12769]
BELLONA OF GLASGOW, Captain Wyllie, from Greenock **with 6
    passengers** bound for Montreal on 4 April 1839; from
    Glasgow to Montreal on 14 August 1839 [SG#8/757; 8/795];
    from Glasgow **with 6 passengers** bound for Canada by 4

April 1842, [GSP#712]; bound for Montreal in July 1842; Captain Auld, arrived in Quebec on 10 May 1846 from Glasgow, [MT]; Captain Auld, from the Clyde to New York on 15 January 1847; Captain Wyllie, from Glasgow to Quebec, arrived there on 3 May 1849; from the Clyde to Montreal on 4 August 1849. [EEC#20396/21451/21814/21845]

BELVIDERA, a 400 ton American ship, Captain Goodman, from Leith to New York in January 1847, arrived in New York on 14 April 1847. [EEC#21445/21499]

BENSON, 1100 tons, Captain Holmes, from Glasgow *with passengers* bound for New York on 1 May 1843. [GSP#799]

BERBICE OF ABERDEEN, a 400 ton barque, master James Elliot, from Aberdeen to Quebec on 12 April 1849; from Aberdeen to Quebec on 6 August 1849; master James Scott, from Aberdeen to Quebec on 11 April 1850, Captain Elliot, from Aberdeen to Quebec on 2 August 1850, from Aberdeen to Quebec on 16 April 1851, arrived there on 24 May 1851; from Aberdeen *with passengers* bound for Quebec on 16 August 1851; master James Scott, from Aberdeen *with passengers* bound for Quebec, arrived there in July 1853. [AJ,18.6.1856]; from Aberdeen *with passengers* bound for Quebec on 26 May 1854; from Aberdeen *with 130 passengers* bound for Canada in August 1854. [Connon MS, Wellington County Museum, Fergus, Ontario] , [AJ#5378/5396/5403/5553] [LCL#3979/3906] [EEC#21797/21847/21955/ 22002/22110 /22452]

BETSEY, Captain Hunter, from Leith *with 121 passengers* bound for Quebec on 18 May 1833, arrived there on 8 July 1833. [LCL#2111][FH#599]

BETTY, a brigantine, Captain Robert Boyd, arrived in Charleston, SC, in July 1833 from Glasgow. [SCGaz#65]

BIRKBY, Captain Hughson, from Leith to St John's on 15 July 1854. [LCL#4318]

BIRMAN, Captain Fuller, from the Clyde to Quebec on 7 July 1851, [EEC#22145]

BIRMINGHAM, 550 tons, Captain Robinson, from Glasgow *with passengers* bound for New York on 28 July 1841. [GSP#673]

BIRNAM, from Isle of Lewis *with 50 passengers* bound for Canada in July 1851; *with 70 passengers from Tiree and 68 passengers from Mull* in July 1851. [GHF#325/326][Argyll Estate Papers#1805, Inveraray]

BITTERN, a brig, from Wick *with passengers* bound for Pictou during 1830

BLACKBURN, a schooner, master Edward Morrison, arrived in Boston
on 19 September 1766 *with 1 passenger* from Scotland.
[PAB]

BLACKNESS, a 266 ton barque, Captain Paton, from Leith *with 44
passengers* bound for Quebec and Montreal in May 1837,
[LCL#2526]; master Andrew Murray from Dundee to Canada
and New York *with 58 passengers* on 29 July 1843,
[BPP.35.503][DW#120]

BLACK NYMPH, Captain Hall, from Aberdeen to Quebec on 13 July
1837, arrived in Quebec 31 August 1837. [AJ#4671/4683]

BLAGDON, Captain Hardie, from Cromarty *with passengers* bound
for Quebec, arrived at Pictou in July 1832, [CP:28.7.1832];
from Leith *with 65 passengers* bound for New York 28 April
1833, arrived there 11 July 1833. [LCL#2105][FH#598]

BLANCHE, from Stornaway, Lewis, *with 453 passengers* bound
for Canada on 26 July 1851 and in 1852. [BPP#68][GHF#325]

BLONDE OF GLASGOW, a 676 ton barque, from Greenock *with
297 passengers* bound for Montreal on 13 May 1843, arrived
there on 19 July 1843; Captain Crawford, from the Clyde to
Quebec on 15 June 1848; from the Clyde to Quebec and
Montreal on 26 May 1849.
[EEC#20627/20632/21670/21816][BPP.35.503]

BOHEMIAN, from Glasgow via Londonderry *with passengers* to
Portland 1 March 1861. [S#1757]

BOLIVAR, a 500 ton barque, Captain Lenius White Duff, from Leith
with passengers bound for Montreal on 15 May 1843.
[EEC#20593]

BOMBAY, 600 tons, from Glasgow to New Orleans on 17 August
1840. [GSP#689]

BONITO, Captain Lybrantz, from the Clyde to New York on 12 April
1850. [EEC#21953]

BONO DEA, 625 tons, from Glasgow to Canada *with 403
passengers* on 4 May 1843, [BPP.35.503]

BOREALIS, Captain Brown, from Greenock to Newfoundland on 14
March 1834, [SG#2/227]; Captain Birnie, from Greenock to
Newfoundland on 4 April 1839. [SG#8/757]

BOSTON, 410 tons, master R. G. Wheatland, from Greenock *with
passengers* to New York in September 1834, arrived in New
York on 9 October 1834. [AJ#4531][GkAd#5008]

BOWES, a brig, Captain Faulkner, from Cromarty *with 172
passengers* bound for Quebec, arrived there on 12 August
1834. [MG]

BREEZE, arrived at Sydney, Cape Breton Island, *with 267
passengers* from Scotland in September 1831.
[PANS.Assembly Mss.Misc.B]

BRIDE, Captain Graham, from the Clyde to Boston on 22 July 1851, [EEC#22151]

BRILLIANT, 550 tons, Captain Alexander Barclay, from Leith to Quebec on 30 July 1829, [LCL#1714]; from Leith *with passengers* bound for Quebec on 24 July 1831; Captain Colburn, arrived in Boston 11 January 1861 from Leith. [EEC#188671][S#1749]

BRILLIANT, a 322 ton brig, from Aberdeen *with 168 passengers* bound for Canada in Spring 1832, [FAO#72]; from Aberdeen *with passengers* bound for Quebec 10 August 1832. [AJ,1.8.1832]; Captain Alexander Duthie, from Dundee to Quebec on 8 August 1833, [FH#597]; from Stromness on 17 June 1834, arrived in Quebec on 8 August 1834, [MG]; from Aberdeen *with 108 passengers* bound for Quebec on 17 August 1834, [AJ#4519]; Aberdeen on 3 April 1835 *with 108 passengers* bound for New York. [FAO#80]; arrived in Quebec on 3 June 1836 from Aberdeen; from Aberdeen *with passengers* bound for Quebec on 11 August 1836; Captain James Elliot, from Aberdeen *with passengers* bound for Quebec in 1 April 1837; from Aberdeen *with passengers* bound for Quebec on 10 August 1837; arrived in Quebec on 14 May 1838 from Aberdeen; from Aberdeen *with passengers* to Quebec on 1 August 1839; from Aberdeen *with 48 passengers* bound for Quebec in April 1840; Captain James Elliot, from Aberdeen to Quebec on 22 July 1840, [AJ#4619/4622/4650/4674/4718/4779/4815/4829]; from Aberdeen to Canada *with 37 passengers* on 17 April 1844, [BPP.35.503][LCL#3250]; Captain Douglas, from Aberdeen to Quebec on 17 April 1851, [LCL#3979]

BRILLIANT, 428 tons, Captain Robert Barr, from Glasgow *with passengers* bound to Montreal *with 191 passengers* on 2 May 1843. [GSP#800][BPP.35.503]; from the Clyde to Quebec *with 217 passengers* on 4 May 1844. [EEC#21039][BPP.35.503]

BRILLIANT, 550 tons, master Alexander Barclay, from Leith to Quebec on 23 July 1830, [LCL#1817]; from Aberdeen *with passengers* bound for Quebec on 10 August 1832. [AJ. 1.8.1832]; Captain Douglas, from Aberdeen to Quebec on 16 April 1851, arrived there on 26 May 1851, [EEC#22110][AJ#5397]

BRITANNIA, from Annan, Dumfries-shire, to Quebec in 1830. [DCr: 13.4.1830]

BRITANNIA, Captain Chambers, from Leith to Quebec *with 16 passengers* on 11 May 1830. [LCL#1788]

BRITANNIA, 104 tons, Captain Coyish, from Port Glasgow to Boston in July 1838. [SG#7/681]

BRITANNIA, 630 tons, Captain Shaw, from Glasgow **with passengers** bound for New York on 3 June 1840; Captain Becket, from Glasgow to St John's, New Brunswick, on 16 June 1842; from Glasgow **with passengers** bound for New York on 10 August 1841. [GSP#676/675/719]

BRITANNIA, from Orkney to Quebec in June 1842. [EEC#20390]

BRITANNIA, Captain Simpson, from Greenock **with passengers** to Quebec on 2 July 1847. [EEC#21523]

BRITANNIA OF GLASGOW, from Glasgow to Montreal in August 1849. [EEC#21855]

BRITISH AMERICA, 663 tons, Captain Joseph Pritchard, from Glasgow **with passengers** bound for Boston on 25 May 1842, *"as the vessels proceeding to the United States are not allowed to carry half the number of passengers in proportion to their tonnage as those proceeding to Quebec and Montreal the accommodations are immensely superior"*; from Glasgow **with passengers** bound for Boston on 18 April 1844. [GSP#849/716]

BRITISH KING, a 240 ton brig, Captain A. Brown, from Leith 15 May 1840 via Cromarty **with 115 passengers (45 from Seaside, Reay) from Caithness** bound for Quebec; Captain Miller, from Dundee to Montreal on 18 August 1849. [S#24/2117][IC,5.8.1840] [EEC#20042/21853/21873][AJ#4827]

BRITISH PRINCESS, Captain Thomson, from Dundee to Quebec on 13 April 1844. [DW#168]

BRITON, Captain Lightfoot, from Montrose to Quebec on 12 April 1849. [EEC#21798]

BRIXTON, Captain Pearson, from Leith to Liverpool, Nova Scotia, on 19 August 1830. [LCL#1824]

BROKE, from Greenock **with 50 passengers** bound for New York on 31 May 1829. [EEC#18339]

BROOKLYN, 500 tons, Captain Richardson, from Glasgow to New York on 12 June 1840; from Glasgow **with passengers** bound for New York on 10 May 1841; from Glasgow **with passengers** bound for New York on 14 July 1842; from Glasgow **with passengers** bound for New York on 1 April 1843. [GSP#662/678/724/779]

BROOKSBY, 505 tons, Captain McEwan, from the Clyde to New York on 9 June 1847, [EEC#21512]; from Glasgow to New York on 16 June 1849; from the Clyde to New York on 4 April 1850, arrived there **with passengers** on 14 May 1850; from Glasgow to New York in August 1850;from the Clyde to New

York on 19 March 1850; from the Clyde **with 285 passengers** to Quebec on 8 July 1851. [SG#18/1824] [GHF#326] [EEC#21825/21950/21971/22023/22097/22145]

BROTHERS, 537 tons, from Glasgow **with passengers** bound for St John's, New Brunswick, on 20 July 1842. [GSP#826]

BROTHERS, 1000 tons, Captain A. Baxter, from Glasgow **with passengers** to New York on 24 June 1849, '**passengers will be supplied with one pound of breadstuff, six pints of water daily, and ten pounds of beef or pork for the journey.**" [EEC#21828][SG#18/1829]

BRUCE, 275 tons, from Glasgow to Quebec on 16 April 1841, [GSP#659]

BRUNSWICK, 414 tons, Captain Hunter, from Glasgow **with passengers** bound for New York on 23 June 1842. [GSP#719]

BRUTUS, 500 tons, from Glasgow to New York on 21 March 1841; from Glasgow to Halifax on 10 October 1841; Captain Jones, from Glasgow **with passengers** bound for New York on 15 May 1842. [GSP#655/683/712]

BUENA VISTA, Captain Mistard, from the Clyde to New York on 1 October 1850; [EEC#22026]

BUENOS AYRES, an American brig, Captain Stuart, from Glasgow **with passengers** bound for New York in May 1840. [S#24/2126]

CALEDONIA, Captain McFarlane, from Alloa **with passengers** bound for Quebec on 5 April 1804. [CM#12880]; from Leith to Quebec on 10 May 1853, [EEC#22431]

CALEDONIA, Captain Greig, from Greenock to Newfoundland on 14 March 1834. [SG#2/227]

CALEDONIA, 500 tons, Captain Knight, from Glasgow **with passengers** bound for New York on 27 July 1842. [GSP#825]

CALEDONIA, 812 tons, Captain Swinford, from Glasgow **with 154 passengers** bound for Quebec on 30 May 1842, **"as the vessels proceeding to the United States are not allowed to carry half the number of passengers in proportion to their tonnage as those proceeding to Quebec and Montreal the accommodations are immensely superior"** [GSP#716];

CALEDONIA, 437 tons, from Glasgow to Canada **with 61 passengers** on 1 August 1843, [BPP.35.503]; from Glasgow to Montreal in March 1845. [EEC#21159]

CALEDONIA, from Glasgow **with 14 passengers** bound for Canada by 4 April 1842. [GSP#712]

CALEDONIA OF GREENOCK, Captain Allan, from the Clyde to
Montreal in July 1842; from the Clyde to Montreal on 17 July
1851. [EEC#20396/222148]

CALEDONIA, 700 tons, Captain Wishart, from Glasgow *with*
passengers bound for St John, New Brunswick, in June 1844.
[GSP#861]

CALEDONIA, 1200 tons, from Glasgow *with passengers* bound for
New York on 25 April 1843. [GSP#799]

CALEDONIA, Captain Greenhorn, from Glasgow *with 13*
passengers bound for Quebec, arrived there on 6 May 1846,
[QG][MT]; from the Clyde to Montreal on 28 March 1849; from
the Clyde to Quebec and Montreal on 2 August 1849,
[EEC#21790/21845]

CALEDONIAN, Captain Hamilton, from the Clyde to Montreal 3 April
1858, [CM#21382]

CALIFORNIA, 629 tons, Captain Auld, from Glasgow *with 327*
passengers, mostly farmers bound for Quebec and
Montreal in June 1842, [FJ#545]; from the Clyde bound for
Quebec *with 328 passengers* on 3 June 1843.
[EEC#20627][BPP.35.503]; Captain Greenhorn, from the Clyde
to Montreal on 27 July 1845, [SG#14/1424]; Captain Lawson,
from the Clyde to St John, New Brunswick, on 3 July 1847.
[EEC#21523]; 468 tons, Captain W. Guthrie, from Glasgow to
Montreal on 11 April 1850, arrived there by 20 May 1850; from
the Clyde to Montreal on 10 August 1850; Captain Gall, from
the Clyde to New Orleans on 15 December 1850; from the
Clyde to Montreal on 11 May 1851; from Glasgow *with 90*
passengers on 25 June 1851;Captain Robert Gall, from
Glasgow *with passengers* bound for Montreal on 7 June
1853; Captain Winter, from the Clyde to Quebec 20 May 1858,
[BPP#68] [EEC#21944/21952/21978/
22004/22058/22120/22439][CM#21419]

CALLAO, Captain Warren, from the Clyde to New Orleans on 19
January 1847. [EEC#21452]

CALLOONEY, a 340 ton barque, master John McConchy, from
Aberdeen to Quebec and Montreal *with passengers* in
August 1844. [DW#183]

CALYPSO, a brig, Captain Gray, from Leith on 11 April 1834 *with 64*
passengers bound for Montreal, arrived there on 17 June
1834. [LCL#2204][MG]

CAMBRIA, 448 tons, Captain John Harrison, from Glasgow *with*
passengers bound for Montreal on 10 July 1848; from
Glasgow *with passengers* bound for Montreal on 29 March
1849; from Glasgow *with passengers* to Montreal on 19 July
1849; from Greenock *with passengers* to Montreal on 17 July

1850; from the Clyde to Montreal on 22 July 1851; Captain
Russell, from the Clyde to Montreal 2 April 1858 [SG#17/1694;
18/1798][CM#21381]
[EEC#21672/21782/21790/21838/21994/22151]
CAMBRIDGE, 800 tons, Captain Bursley, from Glasgow to New York
on 19 June 1840; from Glasgow **with passengers** bound for
New York on 19 October 1841. [GSP#678/684]
CAMBRIDGE, 910 tons, Captain Bouston, from Glasgow **with
passengers** bound for New York on 19 June 1842.
[GSP#719]
CAMBRIDGE, an American ship, Captain Barstow, from Glasgow
with passengers bound for New York on 19 February 1843
and on 19 June 1843. [GSP#791][DW#121]
CAMEO, from the Clyde to Canada in August 1853. [EEC#22479]
CAMILLA, 201 tons, Captain Nicolson, from Leith to St John, New
Brunswick, April 1843. [LCL#3140]
CAMILLUS, from Greenock **with passengers** bound for New York,
arrived there in October 1819. [ANY#2.31]
CAMILLUS, an American ship, master John Niven, from Greenock
with passengers to New York in February 1830,
[GkAd#3424]; from Greenock **with passengers** to New York
in June 1831, [GkAd#3631]; from Greenock **with passengers**
bound for New York on 15 October 1831. [PA#101]; from
Greenock **with passengers** to New York in February 1832,
[GkAd#3706]; from the Clyde to New York during 1833,
[SG#2/156]; from Greenock to New York on 14 March 1834,
[SG#2/227]; from Greenock **with 70 passengers** bound for
New York on 29 July 1834. [SG#3/270]
CANADA, a brig, from Inverness **with passengers** bound for
Quebec, **109 landed** at Pictou in August 1832. [TN:9.8.1832]
CANADA, 300 tons, Captain Allan, from Greenock to Montreal on 27
July 1838; from Greenock **with 55 passengers** bound for
Quebec and Montreal on 31 March 1839; from Greenock to
Quebec and Montreal on 27 July 1839, [SG#7/681; 8/756,
791]; Captain Wilson, from Glasgow to New York on 27 June
1840. [GSP#680]; Captain Allan, from the Clyde to Quebec in
August 1843. [EEC#20651]; Captain McArthur, from the Clyde
to Quebec on 14 July 1847. [EEC#21527]; **with 90
passengers from Barra and South Uist** bound for Canada,
arrived in Quebec during 1848. [GHF#325][TGSI#55.342];
Captain Barclay, from the Clyde to Quebec and Montreal on 27
March 1849, [EEC#21790]; Captain Wyllie, arrived at Montreal
on 22 May 1850 from the Clyde; from the Clyde to Quebec and
Montreal on 12 August 1850. [EEC#21978/22005]; Captain

McGuffie, from the Clyde to Montreal in May 1858,
[CM#21424]

CANADIAN, from Glasgow via Londonderry *with passengers* to
New York 15 February 1861. [S#1757]

CANMORE, Captain Sulye, from the Clyde to Quebec on 2 July 1851,
[EEC#22142]

CANTON, from the Clyde to St John, New Brunswick, in April 1844;
Captain Nicol, from the Clyde to Quebec on 19 July 1849; from
the Clyde to Quebec on 8 April 1851.
[EEC#21017/21838/22106]

CARACTACUS, Captain Jones, from Leith to Quebec 13 August 1860.
[LCL#4953]

CARLO MUARAN, from the Clyde to Philadelphia in February 1853.
[EEC#22411]

CARIBBEAN, from the Clyde *with passengers* bound for St John's,
Newfoundland, foundered in ice off Cape Bollard, passengers
saved, 8 March 1843. [LCL#3153]

CAROLINE, Captain Marsh, from Aberdeen to Quebec on 17 April
1851. [LCL#3979]

CARLTON OF GLASGOW, bound for Miramachi in August 1839.
[EEC#19943];from Glasgow *with passengers* bound for
Quebec 1842. [GA:TD217.24]

CARLTON, Captain Alexander, from Aberdeen to Quebec on 10 April
1848. [EEC#21644]

CARMEN, Captain Laringa, from the Clyde to New Orleans on 14
January 1847. [EEC#21451]

CARNATIC, Captain Devereaux, from the Clyde to New Orleans on
10 February 1853, [EEC#22393]

CAROLINE, 300 tons, Captain Kellam, from Glasgow *with
passengers* bound for Halifax in September 1841. [GSP#681]

CAROLINE, a brig, Captain McComish, from Leith to Montreal on 11
June 1842. [EEC#20374]

CAROLINE OF LONDON, from Peterhead to Quebec on 19 April
1849. [EEC#21801]

CAROLINE, Captain Wyman, from the Clyde to Boston on 24 May
1849. [EEC#21814]

CAROLINE, 600 tons, Captain James March, from Aberdeen *with
passengers* bound for Quebec on 16 April 1840, [AJ#4815];
from Aberdeen to Quebec on 23 April 1849; from Dundee to
Quebec on 4 August 1849, [EEC#21798/21847]; from
Aberdeen to Quebec on 11 April 1850, arrived there on 21 May
1850; from Dundee to Quebec on 27 July 1850.
[EEC#21955/22000] [AJ#5189]; from Dundee via Aberdeen to
Montreal in April 1851, arrived there on 26 May 1851.
[EEC#22120][AJ#5389/5397]

CAROLINE LEISURE, Captain Paton, from the Clyde to St John, New Brunswick, on 17 May 1848. [EEC#21658]

CARRERA, Captain Ritchie, from Aberdeen to Quebec on 17 April 1850, arrived there on 18 May 1850; from Aberdeen to Quebec 12 April 1850 [EEC#21956/21978][LCL#3875]

CARRINGTON, a 100 ton brig, master David Wilson, from Greenock *with passengers* to St John's, Newfoundland, 30 September 1831. [GkAd#3681]

CARROLL OF CARROLLTON, 700 tons, Captain Baird, from Glasgow to New York on 12 May 1840; from Glasgow to New York on 1 October 1840. [GSP#674/693]

CARTHA, a brig, Captain Morrison, from Greenock *with 200 passengers* bound for Quebec in July 1834, arrived at Gross Isle on 29 July 1834, and Quebec on 31 July 1834. [MG]

CASHMERE, Captain Paton, from the Clyde bound for Quebec and Montreal on 18 August 1849, [EEC#21852]; *with passengers from North Uist* bound for Canada, arrived in Quebec in 1849. [GHF#325]

CASPIAN, a 320 ton American ship, Captain David Bartlett, from Glasgow *with passengers* bound for New York on 10 May 1843. [GSP#800]

CASSANDER, 450 tons, Captain Eli Curtis, from Glasgow *with passengers* bound for New York on 25 May 1841. [GSP#666]

CASSANDRA, Captain Rodgers, from Glasgow to New Orleans on 3 November 1839, [SG#8/818]; from the Clyde bound for Dalhousie in June 1843; from the Clyde bound for New Orleans in December 1846; Captain Gall, from the Clyde to Quebec on 15 May 1849; from the Clyde to Quebec on 7 September 1849; Captain Elliot, from the Clyde to Quebec on 4 September 1850. [EEC#20627/21453/21810/21861/22014]

CATHERINE OF IRVINE, arrived in Quebec in May 1833. [SG#2/152]

CATHERINE, 455 tons, Captain Morrison, from Greenock to Quebec on 19 May 1839, [SG#8/771]; from Glasgow to New York on 25 October 1841. [GSP#684]

CATHERINE OF BELFAST, 448 tons, from Islay via Tobermory, Mull, *with 262 passengers from Coll, Knoydart, Arisaig and Eigg* bound for the Gut of Canso, Nova Scotia, 20 July 1843, storm damaged at sea and took refuge in Belfast on 30 August 1843;passengers transferred and arrived at the Gut of Canso and at Quebec in October 1843 on the **JOHN AND ROBERT,** Captain McKechnie. [Mabou Pioneers, p.639, A.MacDonald] [TGSI.55.344][EEC#20650][PANS.CS88.m112]

CATHERINE, Captain Welsh, from the Clyde to Boston on 3 May 1848; from Glasgow to Boston in October 1853. [EEC#21653/22509]

CATHERINE, Captain Flett, from the Clyde to St John's, New Brunswick, on 19 March 1850, arrived there on 25 April 1850; from the Clyde to St John's, New Brunswick, on 17 July 1850. [EEC#21943/21966/21994]

CATHERINE EWAN, Captain Dow, from Dundee to New York on 5 July 1849, [EEC#21834]

CAROLINE, Captain Marsh, from Aberdeen to Quebec on 16 April 1851, [EEC#22110]

CATO, Captain Ritchie, from Dundee to New Orleans on 26 February 1830. [PA#30]

CATO, 460 tons, Captain Bangs Hallet, from Glasgow to Boston on 20 April 1841. [GSP#661]

CERES, Captain Millar, from Dundee to Miramachi on 8 May 1831. [PA#88]

CEYLON, an American ship, Captain E. Cook, from Glasgow *with passengers* bound for New York in July 1844. [GSP#862]

CEYLON, Captain Annandale, from the Shetland Isles to New York in August 1849. [EEC#21861]

CHALLENGE, Captain Crosby, from the Clyde to Boston on 4 July 1849, [EEC#21832]

CHAMPION, 1500 tons, Captain John Cochrane, from Greenock to Dalhousie, New Brunswick, on 10 September 1839, [SG#8/803]; from Glasgow *with passengers* to Quebec and Montreal on 14 June 1849, [SG#18/1826]; from the Clyde to Chaleur Bay on 12 August 1850. [EEC#21823/22005]; Captain Cook, from the Clyde to Quebec in April 1858, [CM#21399]

CHANCELLOR OF GREENOCK, to Quebec in July 1849, [EEC#21834]

CHARLES DE WOLFE, Captain Card, from the Clyde to New York on 8 July 1851, [EEC#22145]

CHARLES FORBES, 500 tons, Captain William Beveridge, from Leith to Miramachi on 3 April 1829, [LCL#1681]; from Leith to Miramachi on 10 April 1830, [LCL#1787]; from Leith to Miramachi on 3 April 1831, [LCL#1889]; from Leith bound for Miramachi on 10 August 1831; from Kirkcaldy *with 50 passengers* bound for Quebec on 1 April 1833. [EEC#18684][FH#574][FJ#4/15]

CHARLES, HENRY, an American ship, from Aberdeen to New Orleans in April 1840. [AJ#4813]

CHARLES HOCKIN, a brig, from Glasgow *with 50 passengers* bound for Pictou, Nova Scotia, in 1833.

CHARLES HUMBERTON, 640 tons, from Tobermory to Canada **with 405 passengers** on 25 July 1843.

CHARLES MCLAUCHLIN, Captain Cain, from the Clyde to Boston on 31 March 1851. [EEC#22102]

CHARLOTTE, a 161 ton brig, master T. Fowlis, arrived in Boston on 29 April 1847 **with 1 passenger** from Glasgow. [USNA#M277/22]

CHARLOTTE, Captain Leslie, from Aberdeen to Quebec on 20 April 1841, [LCL#3459]; Captain Roberts, from Aberdeen to Quebec on 7 July 1847. [EEC#21525]

CHARLOTTE, Captain Vacey, from the Clyde **with 364 passengers from Tiree** bound for Quebec and Montreal on 24 June 1849. [GHF#326][Argyll Estate Papers#1535, Inveraray Castle][EEC#21828]

CHARLOTTE, Captain Fowler, from the Clyde to Boston on 1 July 1849, [EEC#21831]

CHARLOTTE, Captain Fievouz, from the Clyde to Halifax on 8 April 1851, [EEC#22106]

CHARLOTTE HARRISON, a 540 ton barque, Captain Archibald McIntyre, from the Clyde to New York on 25 April 1849, from Greenock **with passengers** to New York on 29 September 1849, [EEC#21802/21870] [SG#18/1853]; from Greenock in May 1850 **with 220 passengers** bound for New York, arrived there in July 1850. [USNA#M237/90] [EEC#21970][NY Daily Tribune,15.7.1850]; from the Clyde to New York on 3 June 1851, [EEC#22130]

CHARLOTTE KERR, a brig, Captain McEachern, from Glasgow probably via Islay and Tobermory **with 50 passengers** bound for Pictou, Nova Scotia, 31 October, 1832, storm damaged returned to Tobermory. landed at Pictou in June 1833. [GkAd#3805][CP:18.6.1833][PANS#282/85]

CHEROKEE, Captain Miller, from Greenock **with 63 passengers** bound for Quebec and Montreal on 16 April 1834, [SG#3/237]; from Grangemouth to Quebec in September 1855.[EEC#788804]

CHERUB, a brig, master John Miller, from Greenock to Montreal in March 1830, from Greenock **with passengers** to Montreal in March 1832. [GkAd#3432/3817]; Captain Welsh, from Greenock **with 24 passengers** bound for Montreal on 27 March 1834. [SG#3/232]

CHESTER, 580 tons, Captain Doyle, from Glasgow **with passengers** bound to New York in September 1842; from Glasgow **with passengers** bound for New York in March 1843; Captain Wilson, from Glasgow **with passengers** bound for New York on 29 March 1844. [GSP#771/779/841]

CHIEFTAIN, Captain Scott, from Leith *with 212 passengers*
bound for Quebec and Montreal in June 1832, [LCL#2011];
arrived in Pictou *with 119 passengers* from   Cromarty on
7 July 1834. [PANS#282/118]

CHIPPEWA OF GLASGOW, a barque, Captain Miller, from the Clyde
with passengers bound for Montreal in August 1839; from
the Clyde on 30 April 1840 *with*
passengers bound for Montreal, passengers and crew mostly
drowned off Cape Rosier on the St Lawrence on 30 April 1840.
[SG#8/791] [EEC#19941/20063]
[AJ#4823]

CHRISTIAN, 300 tons, from Glasgow to Montreal on 1 July   1841.
[GSP#668]; Captain Wallace, from Glasgow and Greenock
with passengers to Quebec on 11 August 1849.
[EEC#21850][SG#18/1846]

CIRCASSIAN, a 350 ton brig, Captain Thomas Ritchie, from
Aberdeen *with passengers* bound for New York on 1 July
1837. [AJ#4658]

CIRCASSIAN, 500 tons, Captain Dixon, from the Clyde to
Quebec on 25 April 1848; from Glasgow *with*
passengers to Montreal and Quebec on 14 June 1849;
Captain Robertson, from Glasgow to New York on 21 April
1850, arrived *with passengers* 22 May 1850.
[EEC#21649/21823/21957][SG#18/1824]

CITY OF ABERDEEN, Captain Munro, arrived in New York in
September 1836 from Dundee, [AJ#4629]; Captain Duffy, from
Glasgow *with passengers* bound for Quebec on 10 July 1842.
[GSP#724]

CITY OF GLASGOW, a 1087 ton steamship, Captain B.R.Matthews,
from Glasgow *with passengers* bound for New York on 14
June 1850. *"Fares: Cabin passage {including Steward's
fee} 20 guineas, 2nd Cabin passage {including
Steward's fee} 12 guineas, no steerage passengers
taken. These rates include provisions but not Wines of
Liquors which will be supplied on board at moderate
prices.";* from the Clyde to New York on 8 August 1850.
[EEC#21969/21981/22003][LCL#3885]

CITY OF QUEBEC, Tulloch, from Aberdeen *with passengers* bound
for Quebec 17 April 1857. [LCL#4607]

CITY OF ROCHESTER, Captain Packman, from Dundee to Quebec 1
May 1850.[LCL#3880]

CITY OF WATERFORD, Captain McGrath, from Glasgow *with*
passengers bound for Quebec on 10 July 1842. [GSP#724]

CLAIRBORNE, 660 tons, Captain Burgess, from Glasgow to   Boston
on 1 June 1841; Captain Roche, from Glasgow *with*

passengers bound for New York on 1 August 1842.
[GSP#666/826]

CLANSMAN, arrived at Sydney, Cape Breton Island, *with over 200 passengers* in September 1836 from Scotland, [PANS#252/88]; Captain Johnston, from the Clyde to Quebec and Montreal on 29 May 1849; Captain Fordyce, from the Clyde to Montreal on 8 June 1850; Captain Robertson, from the Clyde to Quebec on 13 June 1851. [EEC#21817/21978/22135]

CLARE, Captain Allan, arrived in Boston on 19 April 1851 from the Clyde; from the Clyde to Boton in April 1853; from the Clyde to Boston in May 1854; Captain Carruthers, from Dumfries to Quebec, 31 March 1858.[EEC#22117/22591/22428] [CM#21381]

CLARENCE, from the Clyde to Boston in April 1848; Captain Armstrong, from the Clyde to Boston on 30 August 1849. [EEC#21656/21855]

CLARINDA, Captain Cameron, from Aberdeen to Quebec in September 1858, [CM#21388]; from Aberdeen to Quebec on 27 March 1860. [AJ#5855]

CLARISSA ANDREWS, 474 tons, Captain Colby, from Glasgow *with passengers* bound for New Orleans on 21 March 1844. [GSP#841]

CLEOPATRA, Captain Morris, from Cromarty bound for Quebec in August 1831. [EEC#18684]

CLEOSTRATUS, a barque, from Glasgow *with 64 passengers* bound for Pictou, Nova Scotia, in 1842. [AH:30.4.1842][GH:18.4.1842]

CLIFTON, 614 tons, Captain Ingersoll, from Glasgow *with passengers* to New York on 25 September 1842. [GSP#771]

CLIO, Captain Young, from Leith *with 41 passengers* to New York 6 April 1836, [LCL#2412]; from Leith and Cromarty *with passengers* bound for New York in 1836. [AJ,16.3.1836]

CLUTHA OF GREENOCK, 498 tons, Captain Cronk, from Greenock *with 5 passengers* bound for St John, New Brunswick, on 24 August 1839, [SG#8/798]; to St Johns, New Brunswick, in March 1840, [EEC#20037]; Captain Thomas Callendar, from Glasgow *with passengers* bound for New York on 24 April 1841. [GSP#661]; Captain Fowler, from Glasgow *with passengers* to New York on 20 April 1848, [SG#17/1703]; Captain Laing, arrived in New York from Glasgow in 1849, [SG#18/1834]; Captain Muir, from the Clyde to New York on 2 May 1850; from the Clyde to Quebec on 28 May 1851. [EEC#21646/21963/22127]

CLYDE, a brig, from Greenock, *with 14 passengers* to Nova Scotia, landed at Halifax in April 1832. [TN:26.4.1832]; Captain

Nicholson, from the Clyde to Quebec in April 1840. [EEC#20045]

CLYDESDALE, Captain Thomas Auld, from Glasgow *with passengers* bound for Halifax, Nova Scotia, on 20 March 1848. [SG#17/1699]

COBEQUID, from the Clyde to Boston in June 1853. [EEC#22464]

COLLINGWOOD, Captain Guthrie, from Troon to Quebec on 11 April 1848; from Ayr to Quebec on 10 April 1849; from Ayr to Quebec on 2 August 1849; from Troon to Quebec on 11 April 1850. [EEC#21645/21796/21845/21955]

COLOSUS, 393 tons, Captain Lennox, from Glasgow *with passengers* bound for New York on 1 August 1844. [GSP#867]

COLUMBIA, from Leith to Quebec in July 1843. [EEC#20639]

COLUMBIA, Captain Hay, from Ardrossan to Quebec on 6 April 1850, arrived there on 18 May 1850. [EEC#21951/21978]

COLUMBUS, a 305 ton brig, Captain Low, from Leith to Miramachi on 8 April 1830; Captain Robert Pearson, from Leith to Restigouche on 30 March 1834; from Leith *with passengers* bound for Miramachi on 30 March 1839; Captain Pearson, from Leith to Dalhousie in April 1840; from Leith to Miramachi on 3 April 1841; from Leith to Miramachi 6 April 1843; from Leith to Miramachi in April 1844.[FJ#66] [EEC#19875/21017][LCL#1786/3454/

COLUMBUS, a 610 ton American ship, from Glasgow to New York on 19 July 1840; from Glasgow to New York on 7 March 1841; Captain Cole, from Glasgow *with passengers* bound for New York on 7 July 1842; from Glasgow *with passengers* bound for New York on 19 March 1843 and on 19 July 1843; Captain Sanders, from the Clyde to New York on 14 March 1850. [GSP#655/681/723/791][EEC#22096][DW#121]

COMMERCE, Captain Wyse, from Glasgow to New York on 6 October 1838. [SG#7/708]

COMMODORE, Captain Pritchard, from the Clyde to New York on 29 May 1849. [EEC#21817]

COMMODORE, Captain Low, from Montrose to Quebec on 25 April 1849. [EEC#21803]

COMMODORE NAPIER, Captain Casson, from the Clyde to Richmond, Virginia, on 14 January 1847. [EEC#21451]

COMPETITOR, Captain Goudey, from the Clyde to Boston on 25 June 1850; Captain Trefrey, from the Clyde to Boston on 24 February 1853. [EEC#21985/22401]

COMPTON, 547 tons, Captain Chapman, from Glasgow *with passengers* bound for Quebec and Montreal in April 1843. [GSP#779]

CONCORD, Captain Potter, from the Clyde to Montreal on 4 April 1851, [EEC#22105]

CONDUCTION, from the Clyde to Boston in July 1854. [EEC#22616]

CONFERENCE, Captain Buchan, from Leith *with 122 passengers* to Quebec and Montreal 28 May 1834, [LCL#2218]; arrived in Quebec on 28 July 1834 *with 142 passengers* from Leith. [AJ#4522][MG]

CONGRESS, 270 tons, Captain Portman, from Glasgow *with passengers* to New York on 17 July 1841. [GSP#668/673]

CONQUEROR, from Leith to Montreal in April 1844. [EEC#21017]

CONRAD, Captain Barclay, from the Clyde to New York on 21 April 1849, from the Clyde to Mobile on 15 October 1849, [EEC#21801/21876]; from the Clyde to Quebec on 18 June 1850, [EEC#21982]; Captain Kelso, from the Clyde to New York on 20 November 1850, [EEC#22046]; *with 241 passengers, 167 from Tiree and 74 from Mull* bound for Canada in 1850; Captain Kelso, from the Clyde *with 389 passengers from Tiree* bound for Quebec in July 1851. [GHF#326][Argyll Estate Papers#1804/1805, Inveraray Castle][EEC#22145]

CONSTELLATION, Captain McFie, from the Clyde to Quebec on 28 July 1849, [EEC#21843]

CONSTITUTION, 558 tons, Captain Neill, from Glasgow *with passengers* bound for Quebec on 10 April 1843. [GSP#779/800]

CORDELIA, Captain Love, from the Clyde to Newfoundland on 2 August 1845, [SG#14/1426]; Captain Wallace, from the Clyde to Newfoundland on 29 August 1850. [EEC#22012] from the Clyde to Providence in August 1853. [EEC#22492]

CORDELIA OF WINDSOR, NOVA SCOTIA, a brig, from Glasgow to Halifax, Nova Scotia, in September 1854. [EEC#22645]

CORIALANUS, an American ship, Captain L. W. Merrill, from Greenock *with passengers* bound for New York on 5 August 1837. [AJ#4672]

CORNELIA, 1115 tons, Captain French, from Glasgow *with passengers* bound for New York on 1 June 1843, [DW#121]; from Glasgow *with passengers* bound for New York on 23 July 1844. [GSP#866]

CORLINA, Captain Young, from the Clyde to New York on 9 March 1849. [EEC#21783]

COROMADO, 646 tons, from Glasgow to Boston in March 1841. [GSP#654]

CORRA LINN, a 1600 ton U.S Line ship, Captain F. M. Lambert, from the Clyde to New York on 26 May 1849; from Glasgow *with passengers* to New York on 8 October 1849; from the Clyde to New York on 4 March 1850; from the Clyde to New York on 1 July 1850; Captain Duane, arrived in New York on 19 April 1851 from the Clyde; Captain Lambert, from the Clyde to New York on 5 July 1851; from the Clyde to New York on 29 January 1853. [SG#18/1860][EEC#21816/ 21874/ 21936/21987/22117/22144/22389]

CORSAIR OF GREENOCK, a 450 ton brig, Captain Scott, arrived in Prince Edward Island on 19 May 1830 *with 206 passengers* from Greenock. [TIM#17.33]; from Greenock *with 30 passengers and heads of families* bound for Nova Scotia, arrived at the Gut of Canso on 11 September 1830, [CP:2.10.1830]; from Leith via Cromarty *with passengers* bound for Pictou and Quebec on 17 June 1831. [EEC#18628/18649/18661]; arrived in Pictou *with 161 passengers* bound for Quebec in August 1831, [CP:20.8.1831]; Captain Ritchie, from the Clyde to Quebec in 1833, [SG#2/170]; arrived in Halifax *with 3 passengers* on 31 May 1833, [PANS#282/81]; from Lochmaddy *with passengers* bound for Cape Breton in July 1838. [TGSI#55.342]; arrived in Sydney, Cape Breton Island, on 4 September 1838 *with 155 passengers* from Tobermory, [PANS#338/72; 252/147]; Captain Nicol, from the Clyde to Quebec on 1 August 1849, [EEC#21844]

COVERDALE, Captain Benson, from Grangemouth to Quebec on 20 April 1848. [EEC#21648]

CRAIGIEVAR, a 260 ton brig, Captain Barclay, from Dundee to New York and Richmond, Virginia, on 1 May 1840. [EEC#20042][S#24/2117]

CREDO, from Aberdeen to Quebec in August 1850. [EEC#22032]

CRESCENT, Captain Balls, from Glasgow to Boston on 13 July 1839, [SG#8/786]; Captain Nickerson, from the Clyde to Boston on 30 March 1849. [EEC#21792]

CROWN, a 338 ton brig, Captain Howie, from Greenock *with passengers* to Pictou in March 1831, [GkAd#3626]; Captain McAlpin, from the Clyde to Quebec, arrived there in June 1833. [SG#2/158]

CRUIKSTON CASTLE, Captain McKinley, from Greenock *with 41 passengers* bound for Quebec on 5 April 1839, [SG#8/759]

CUMBERLAND, arrived in Sydney, Nova Scotia, *with 106 passengers* from Scotland by September 1831. [PANS.Assembly Mss.Misc.B]

CUMBERLAND OF MARYPORT, from Kirkcudbright to Richibucto in June 1832. [CM#17326]
CUMBRIA, *with 17 passengers from Mull and Tiree* bound for Canada in 1850. [GHF#326][Argyll Estate Papers#1804, Inveraray Castle]
CUMMING, 545 tons, Captain Salter, from Glasgow to New York on 9 April 1841, [GSP#659]
CUNARD, from the Clyde to Quebec in August 1853. [EEC#22481]
CUTHBERTS, Captain Sangster, from the Clyde to New York on 2 April 1849. [EEC#21792]
CYBELE, Captain Greig, from Dundee to St John's, New Brunswick, on 23 March 1849. [EEC#21789]
CYGNET, Captain Nairn, from the Clyde to St John's, New Brunswick, on 4 June 1850. [EEC#21976]
CYNTHIA, Captain Goldsworthy, from the Clyde to Newfoundland on 4 May 1847; from Ardrossan to New Providence, Rhode Island, in July 1853. [EEC#21497/22468]
CYRUS, Captain Scott, from Leith *with 32 passengers* to Quebec/Montreal 10 April 1835, [LCL#2302]; arrived in Quebec on 18 May 1834 from Dundee. [AJ#4512]
CZAR, a brig, Captain Russell, from Greenock *with over 100 passengers* bound for New York on 11 July 1829. [EEC#18357]; from Greenock *with 110 passengers* bound for New York in July 1834. [MG]
CZAR, Captain Muir, from Dundee via Longhope, Orkney, to St John, New Brunswick, in April 1848; Captain Smellie, from Dundee to Quebec on 17 July 1850; from Dundee to St John, New Brunwick in February 1853. [EEC#21645/21995/22407]
DAEDELUS, Captain Scott, from Leith to Miramachi on 4 April 1829, [LCL#1680]; from Leith to Miramachi on 3 April 1830, [LCL#1785]; from Leith to Miramachi in March 1831, [LCL#1887]; Captain Gavin, from Leith *with 90 passengers* to New York 26 April 1834, [LCL#2209]; arrived in New York in 1834 from Leith. [AJ#4515]
DAHLIA, 1004 tons, Captain Porter, from the Clyde to Boston on 16 August 1849; master G. D. Taste, from Greenock *with passengers* bound for Quebec and Montreal in July 1854. [EEC#21850][AJ#5556]
DALMARNOCK, a 315 ton brig, master Archibald McFarlane, from Leith *with passengers* bound for Quebec on 1 April 1831. [EEC#18612]; from the Clyde to New York, arrived there in June 1833, [SG#2/158]; from Leith *with 110 passengers* to New York 11 April 1834, [LCL#2204]; from Greenock *with passengers* bound for New York on 20 September 1834.

[AJ#4518]; Captain Burns, from the Clyde to New Richmond on 19 July 1845, [SG#14/1422]

DALMATIA, from Greenock *with 41 passengers* bound for New York in Spring 1832. [CM#17337]

DAMARISCOTTA, Captain Howes, from Dundee to Philadelphia on 19 September 1849. [LCL#3816] [EEC#21866]

DAMASCUS, 600 tons, Captain Bliss, from Glasgow to Boston on 20 June 1842. [GSP#719]

DARING, Captain Waterbing, from the Clyde to St John's on 7 September 1849. [EEC#21861]

DAVID GRANT, a 300 ton brig, Captain George Lawrence, from Leith to Montreal in April 1841, [LCL#3458]; from Leith via Dundee *with passengers* bound for Quebec and Montreal on 16 April 1846. [EEC#21331][DPCA#2321]

DEBORAH, Captain Ellis, from the Clyde to Quebec on 16 March 1850. [EEC#22096]

DEFENCE, Captain Rogers, from Leith to Miramachi on 13 August 1829, [LCL#1715]; from Leith to Miramachi on 19 August 1830, [LCL#1824]; from Leith bound for Miramachi on 9 August 1831. [EEC#18684]

DEFENDER, Captain Vowell, from the Clyde to Montreal on 26 June 1851. [EEC#22140]

DENMARK, 554 tons, Captain Frost, from Glasgow *with passengers* bound for New York on 24 March 1844. [GSP#841]

DEVERON, a 333 ton brigantine, master Thomas Edington, from Greenock *with passengers* to New Orleans in 1832, [GkAd#3706]; Captain Cameron, from Greenock to Quebec on 23 June 1838, [SG#7/673]; Captain MacLean, from Lochinver *with 140 passengers from Croick and Assynt, Sutherland,* bound for Pictou, Nova Scotia, in 1840. [IC,7.10.1840]

DIADEM, 460 tons, Captain Lambert, from Glasgow to New York on 11 June 1840. [GSP#673]

DIAMOND, Captain Mann, from the Clyde to Baltimore on 8 April 1851, [EEC#22106]

DIANA, a 200 ton brig, Captain Millar, from Leith to Richibucto on 7 April 1829, [LCL#1786]; from Glencaple, Dumfries-shire, to St John, New Brunswick, in 1831, [DCr: 3.1.1831]; from Leith *with 5 passengers* to Quebec in September 1832, [CM#17337][LCL#2039]; Captain Wilkie, from Leith to New Brunswick 13 April 1840, [LCL]; from Leith *with passengers* bound for Halifax and St John, New Brunswick, on 20 March 1841. [EEC#20163]

DIANA OF GREENOCK, a brig, Captain Gray, bound for Newfoundland in May 1843, [EEC#20607]; from the Clyde bound for Newfoundland in July 1844. [GSP#870]

DIANA, a brig, from Glencaple, Dumfries-shire, to St John's, New Brunswick, 1831, [DCr: 3.1.1831]; master Robert Cowan, from Glencaple Quay to Quebec in 1833. [DC, 26.3.1833]

DIANA OF DUMFRIES, Captain Edgar, to Quebec in April 1840; from Dumfries to Quebec on 28 March 1849; Captain Chambers, from Dumfries to Quebec on 3 April 1851. [EEC#20047/21792/22105]

DIDO OF BOSTON, a brig, from Leith bound for New York on 18 December 1830. [EEC#18594]

DILIGENCE, Captain Kirk, from Leith *with 55 passengers* to Quebec and Montreal 9 June 1833, [LCL#2117]

DISRAELI, Captain Weeks, from the Clyde to Montreal on 23 April 1851. [EEC#22112]

DOLPHIN, from Glasgow to Montreal in June 1844. [EEC#21050]

DOMUS, from Peterhead bound for Canada in 1835, [AJ]

DON, 440 tons, Captain Muir, from Glasgow to Quebec in March 1841; from Glasgow *with passengers* bound for Quebec and Montreal in April 1843. [GSP#654/779]

DORCHESTER, 500 tons, Captain Caldwell, from Glasgow *with passengers* bound for Boston on 24 July 1844. [GSP#86]

DOUGLAS, 634 tons, Captain McKennel, from Leith to St Johns on 6 June 1841, [LCL#3472]

DOUGLAS, a 376 ton barque, Captain William Mellon, from Leith *with passengers* bound for Quebec on 1 August 1853. [EEC#22467][LCL#4214]

DROMNAHAIR OF SLIGO, a barque, Captain Pyne, from the Clyde bound for Montreal on 20 April 1844, went ashore on Crane Island on 10 June 1844, later arrived at Quebec. [GSP#86]; Captain Pyne, from the Clyde to New York on 19 February 1853. [EEC#22398]

DUCHESS OF KENT, Captain Wilson, from the Clyde to New York on 13 September 1849. [EEC#21863]

DUCHESS OF RENFREWSHIRE, from the Clyde to St John, New Brunswick, in March 1851. [EEC#22105]

DUKE, Captain Welch, from the Clyde to Quebec on 15 April 1850, arrived there on 18 May 1850; from the Clyde *with emigrants* bound for Quebec in July 1854.[LCL#4327] [EEC#21954/21978/22621]

DUKE OF CORNWALL, Captain Ronald, from Ardrossan to St John's, New Brunswick, on 16 December 1846, possibly lost at sea. [EEC#21506]

DUNBARTON, Captain Cole, from Greenock to St John, Newfoundland, in January 1860. [DC#23464]

DUNDEE, from Dundee to New York in June 1842. [EEC#20381]

DUNDONALD, 190 tons, from Irvine to Canada *with 9 passengers* on 14 June 1843, [BPP.35.503]

DURHAM, Captain Taylor, from the Clyde to Boston on 24 March 1849. [EEC#21789]

DWINA, from Peterhead *with passengers* bound for Canada in 1832; Captain Volum, at Quebec on 5 June 1834 from Peterhead. [AJ#4514]

E. SWAN, from Glasgow to Baltimore in July 1860. [DC#23523]

EAGLE, a 307 ton barque, Captain W. Lang, from Glasgow *with passengers* bound for Pictou in 1842; from Glasgow to Canada *with 91 passengers* on 18 April 1843, [BPP.35.503]; from Glasgow *with passengers* bound for Boston on 17 August 1843. [GSP#779][EEC#20639]

EARL GREY, a brig, Captain William Douglas, from Leith *with passengers* bound for Montreal on 1 April 1842. [EEC#20330]

EARL OF DALHOUSIE, a 222 ton brig, Captain James Boyd, from Glasgow *with passengers* bound for Montreal on 20 March 1834. [SG#3/225]

EARL OF FIFE, from Stornaway *with 20 passengers* bound for Nova Scotia, landed at Sydney, Cape Breton Island, on 5 August 1832. [PANS#282/48]

EARL OF HOPTOUN OF ABERDEEN, Captain Bartlett, from Aberdeen to Sydney, Cape Breton, in April 1844. [LCL#3251]

EARL PERCY, 319 tons, Captain John Gordon, from Leith *with passengers* bound for Quebec on 30 April 1839. [EEC#19877]

EARL POWIS, Captain Walker, from Dundee to Montreal on 31 March 1849; from Dundee to Quebec on 29 March 1850, arrived in Montreal on 27 May 1850; from Dundee to Montreal on 19 August 1850; from Dundee to Montreal on 1 April 1851. [EEC#21792/21948/21978/22008/22105]

EBAN PREBBLE, a 600 ton American ship, Captain Hinckley, from Glasgow *with passengers* bound for New Orleans on 22 September 1842. [GSP#771]

EBRO, from Glasgow to Charleston in July 1849, [EEC#21844]

EBOR, Captain Smith, from Montrose to Quebec 8 April 1840. [LCL]

ECHO, Captain Steele, from Cromarty to Quebec on 28 April 1851. [EEC#22116]

ECLIPSE, arrived in Sydney, Cape Breton Island, *with 100 passengers* from Tobermory, Mull, in 1837. [PANS#338/72; 252/127]

ECLIPSE, Captain Sedgwick, from the Clyde to Boston on 5 July 1850. [EEC#21990]

ECONOMIST, a barque, Captain Stocombe, from Leith *with 42 passengers* bound to Pictou on 12 August 1833. [FH#603][PANS#282/85]

EDINA, Captain Simpson, from the Clyde to Quebec on 12 July 1845, [SG#14/1420]

EDINBURGH, a 283 ton American ship, Captain F. R. Theobald, from Glasgow *with passengers* bound for New York on 10 July 1839, [SG#8/779, 787]

EDINBURGH, 870 tons, Captain Lawson, from Glasgow *with passengers* to Quebec on 20 June 1842; Captain Jack, from Glasgow *with passengers* bound for Quebec and Montreal on 6 April 1843. [GSP#719/723/796]

EDINBURGH, a 2400 ton steamship, Captain William Cumming, from Glasgow *with passengers* bound for New York on 26 December 1855, [EEC#788804]; from Glasgow *with passengers* bound for New York on 20 February 1856, [CM#20703][FJ#1203]; from Glasgow on 19 April 1856 *with passengers* bound for New York, arrived in New York *with passengers* on 6 May 1856.[ScotGen#44.1.40][FJ#1210]; from Glasgow *with passengers* bound for New York 18 June 1856, [FJ#1219]; arrived in New York 12 May 1858 from the Clyde, [CM#21424]

EDMOND PERKINS, 662 tons, Captain Ingersoll, from Glasgow *with passengers* bound for New York on 8 August 1842. [GSP#826]

EDWIN, Captain Stewart, from Leith bound for New York in May 1832. [LCL#2007]

EGERTON, Captain Henderson, from Dundee to Quebec on 31 March 1849; Captain Moore, from Dundee to New York on 11 March 1850; from Dundee to St John's, New Brunswick, on 2 September 1850. [S#3151/3531][EEC#21792/21940/22013]

EGLINTON, 987 tons, from Greenock *with passengers* bound for Canada in April 1847; from Greenock *with passengers* bound for New York on 31 May 1842. [GSP#715]

ELBE, Captain Heydemann, from the Clyde to New York on 24 February 1853. [EEC#22401]

ELDON, 104 tons, master John McAlpin, from Greenock *with passengers* to Chaleur Bay, New Brunswick, in April 1830, [GkAd#3435]; from Greenock *with passengers* to New york in Fenruary 1832, [GkAd#3814]; from Skye *with 250 passengers* bound for Quebec in Spring 1832. [CM#17337]; from Tobermory, Mull, *with 121 passengers,* landed at Sydney, Cape Breton Island, on 10 September 1832. [PANS#282/48]

ELEUTHERA, 423 tons, from Glasgow to Canada *with 160 passengers* on 19 May 1843, [BPP.35.503]

ELI WHITNEY, 500 tons, Captain Eli Harding, from Glasgow *with passengers* bound for Boston on 6 August 1842. [GSP#826]; from the Clyde to New York in September 1853. [EEC#22505]

ELIZA, Captain Hynd, from Dundee to New York on 10 May 1830. [PA#42]

ELIZA, Captain Hamilton jr., from Greenock *with 14 passengers* bound for Chaleur Bay on 4 April 1834. [SG#3/234]

ELIZA, Captain Morgan, from Aberdeen to Quebec on 2 May 1841, [LCL#3462]; from Aberdeen to Quebec in June 1846. [AJ#5142]

ELIZA, *with around 140 passengers from Tiree* bound for Canada in 1847.[GHF#326][Argyll Estate Papers# 1533, Inveraray Castle]

ELIZA, 307 tons, Captain McEwan, from Greenock *with 42 passengers* bound for Quebec and Montreal on 18 June 1838, [SG#7/673-7]; Captain Grange, from Glasgow to Montreal on 18 April 1839, [SG#8/763]; from Irvine to Canada *with 12 passengers* on 10 April 1843, [BPP.35.503]; Captain Brown, from Troon to Quebec on 5 April 1848; from Troon to Quebec on 10 April 1849; from Troon to Quebec on 23 July 1849; from Troon to Dalhousie, New Brunswick, on 11 April 1850; from Irvine to Quebec in September 1850. [EEC#21644/21797/21841/21953/22027]

ELIZA, Captain Durkie, from the Clyde to Boston on 23 October 1850. [EEC#22034]

ELIZA ANN, Captain Breen, from the Clyde to St John, New Brunswick, on 24 July 1845. [SG#14/1423]

ELIZA HALL, Captain Rennie, from Aberdeen to Sydney, Cape Breton Island, on 5 June 1850. [EEC#21977]

ELIZA SWIFT, Captain Lewis, from the Clyde to New York on 18 August 1849. [EEC#21852]

ELIZA WARWICK, 540 tons, Captain Davis, from Glasgow to Baltimore in March 1841, [GSP#653]

ELIZABETH, master A. Grierson, arrived in New Orleans on 12 November 1827 *with 5 passengers* from Glasgow. [USNA/par]

ELIZABETH, Captain Morrison, from Leith to New Brunswick on 2 April 1831; from Leith *with 14 passengers* to Montreal 28 June 1833. [LCL#1889/2105]

ELIZABETH, a 226 ton brig, Captain Stocks, from Kirkcaldy to Bathurst on 3 April 1840; Captain Ovenstone, from Leith to Halifax in June 1841; Captain James Stocks, from Leith *with 185 passengers* bound for Montreal on 13 April 1842;

Captain Ovenstone, from Leith to Halifax in April 1845.
[EEC#20339][GSP#712] [LCL#3353/3471]

ELIZABETH, Captain Anderson, from Glasgow **with passengers** bound for New York on 29 March 1842. [GSP#710]

ELIZABETH, 610 tons, Captain Bruce, from Glasgow **with passengers** bound for Quebec and Montreal on 15 April 1843. [GSP#799]

ELIZABETH, Captain Laurence, from the Clyde to New York on 20 April 1848. [EEC#21649]

ELIZABETH OF SOUTH SHIELDS, a brig, from the Clyde to Quebec in July 1837. [CM#18300]

ELIZABETH OF YARMOUTH, NOVA SCOTIA, a brig, Captain Scott, from Ardrossan to Boston, wrecked on Scituate Beach on 19 January 1855. [EC#22696]

ELIZABETH, Captain Bently, from Glasgow to New York in July 1854. [EEC#22624]

ELIZABETH, Captain Brown, from the Clyde to Montreal 10 June 1858, [CM#21410]

ELIZABETH MARGARET, Captain Duthie, from the Clyde to Newfoundland on 19 June 1849. [EEC#21826]

ELIZABETH ROSE, a 250 ton brig, from Leith **with passengers** bound for Quebec and Montreal on 30 March 1849 (27 April 1849?); Captain William Fordyce, from Leith **with passengers** bound for Quebec and Montreal in April 1851. [EEC#21767/21804/22088][LCL#3977]

ELLEN, 550 tons, from Leith bound for Quebec on 28 May 1831. [EEC#18643]

ELLEN OF LIVERPOOL, a 380 ton barque, master Dugald McLachlan, from Loch Laxford **with 158 passengers** bound for Pictou, Nova Scotia, on 22 May 1848, arrived there on 30 June 1848. [PANS#RG1.257.110][PB#108/110]

ELLEN, Captain Haggart, from the Clyde to Newfoundland on 26 June 1849, [EEC#21829]

ELLEN BROOKES, 464 tons, Captain Heries, from Glasgow to Boston in July 1841. [GSP#668]

ELLEN BRYSON, a 554 ton barque, Captain Peter Clark, from Greenock **with 7 passengers** bound for St John, New Brunswick, on 24 September 1839; Captain Bryson, from Glasgow to St John, New Brunswick, on 2 May 1839, [SG#8/765; 8/797; 8/808]; from the Clyde to St John's, New Brunswick, in October 1840. [GSP#646]

ELLEN DOUGLAS OF ANNAN, to Quebec in August 1849. [EEC#21851]

ELLENGOWAN, a brig, master James Cappon, from Dundee to New York in July 1844. [DW#171]

ELLERSLIE, Captain Harvey. from Alloa via Leith to Quebec on 3
August 1849; from the Clyde to Norfolk in September 1855.
[EEC#21865/21847/788804]

EMERALD, Captain Leslie, from Dundee to New York on 10 August
1830. [PA#54]

EMERALD, 350 tons, Captain Carter, from Glasgow *with
passengers* bound for Charleston and Savannah on 5 October
1841. [GSP#683/684]

EMIGRANT, from Montrose *with passengers* bound for Canada in
1856. [AJ,11.6.1856]

EMILY OF LEITH, Captain Anderson, from Leith to San Francisco
oon 25 March 1853. [EEC#22499][LCL#4182]

EMILY, a barque, from Troon to Quebec in October 1855.
[EEC#788813]

EMMA OF DUNDEE, 211 tons, from Dundee *with passengers* to
New York in June 1835. [FJ#130]; Captain Young, arrived in
Sydney, Cape Breton, on 5 May 1838 from Dundee and
Aberdeen, [AJ#4723]; Captain Alexander Innes, from Dundee
to Montreal *with 34 passengers* on 4 April 1843, [DW#107]
[BPP.35.503]; from Dundee to Montreal *with passengers* in
April 1844, [DW#157]; Captain Christie, from Dundee to
Quebec on 18 April 1848. [EEC#21646]

EMMA, 211 tons, Captain Young, from Leith to Montreal on 22 July
1837, [CM#18297]; Captain Innes, from Leith to Montreal in
April 1844. [EEC#21017][LCL#3352]

EMMA SEARLE, Captain Hescroft, from the Clyde to New York on 27
February 1849. [EEC#21778]

EMPRESS, a 360 ton barque, Captain Leslie, from Banff, via
Scrabster Roads, Caithness, and Stromness, Orkney, *with
passengers* bound for Quebec in April 1851.
[AJ#5376/5389/5390][EEC#22112]

ENGLAND, 893 tons, Captain Johnstone, from Glasgow *with
passengers* bound for Quebec on 5 May 1843,
[GSP#800]; from Glasgow *with passengers* bound for
Quebec on 20 June 1844. [GSP#861]

ENGLAND, a 713 ton American ship, from Glasgow *with
passengers* bound for New York on 7 August 1840;
Captain Waite, from Glasgow *with passengers* bound for
New York on 7 August 1841; Captain Lowber, from Glasgow
with passengers bound for New York on 19 April 1843 and
on 19 August 1843; Captain Bartlett, from Glasgow *with
passengers* bound for New York on 1 August 1844.
[GSP#685/867/791][DW#121]

ENGLAND, 413 tons, from Glasgow to Mobile on 21 October 1841.
[GSP#684]

ENTAW, 629 tons, from Glasgow to Canada **with 54 passengers** on 30 August 1843, [BPP.35.503]

ENTERPRISE OF LIVERPOOL, from the Bay of Tarbet, Harris, **with 381 passengers** bound for Cape Breton Island on 6 July 1842. [EEC#20390]

ENTERPRISE, Captain Patterson, from the Clyde to New York on 1 June 1850. [EEC#21975]

ENVOY, Captain McKettrick, from the Clyde to Mobile on 22 January 1847; Captain Patton, from the Clyde to Philadelphia on 25 February 1850; from the Clyde to Quebec in August 1850; from the Clyde to Mobile in November 1854; Captain McAlpine, from the Clyde to Dalhousie, 8 April 1858. [CM#21385] [EEC#21454/21933/22023/22679]

ENVOY OF GREENOCK, a barque, from Greenock to Quebec in August 1855. [EEC#322788]

ERROMANGA, a 394 ton bark, from Glasgow to Montreal in March 1845, [EEC#21159]; Captain Robert Ramsay, from Glasgow **with 13 passengers** bound for Quebec, arrived there on 6 May 1846, [QG][MT]; from Glasgow **with passengers** to Quebec on 19 April 1848, [EEC#21645][SG#17/1694]; **with 60 passengers from Barra and South Uist** bound for Canada, arrived in Quebec during 1848. [GHF#325]; from Glasgow **with passengers** bound for Montreal in March 1849; from the Clyde to Quebec and Montreal on 2 August 1849; arrived in Montreal on 6 May 1850 from the Clyde; from the Clyde to Montreal on 21 March 1850.[SG#18/1798] [EEC#21782/21845/21971/22099]

ESSEX, 330 tons, Captain Raynes, from Glasgow **with passengers** bound for Boston on 28 April 1843. [GSP#799]

ESTHER, Captain Duffus, from Dundee to St John, New Brunswick, on 12 April 1848. [EEC#21645]

EUCLID OF LIVERPOOL, 500 tons, Captain G. Bainbridge, from Broomielaw, Glasgow, **with around 300 passengers from Islay and Kintyre** bound for Quebec in July 1847.[North British Daily Mail, 21.7.1847] [AJ#5184/5188]; from Glasgow to Quebec on 7 April 1851, [EEC#22105/22120]

EUPHEMIA, Captain Gowans, from the Clyde to Newfoundland on 28 July 1849; from the Clyde to Newfoundland on 15 May 1850; from the Clyde to Newfoundland on 17 July 1850; Captain McLean, from the Clyde to Newfoundland on 30 September 1850. [EEC#21843/21967/21994/22024]

EUROPE, a 600 ton American ship, Captain Marshall, from Glasgow **with passengers** bound for New York on 27 May 1840; from Glasgow **with passengers** bound for New York on 19 September 1840; from Glasgow **with passengers** bound for

New York on 19 September 1841; Captain Marshall, from
Glasgow *with passengers* bound for New York on 19
September 1842; Captain Furber from Glasgow *with
passengers* bound for New York on 19 May 1843 and on 19
September 1843. [GSP#676/690/682/771/791]

EUROPE, from Dundee to New York in May 1835. [FJ#131]

EUROPEAN, 526 tons, Captain Scott, from Leith *with 54
passengers* to Quebec and Montreal 25 April 1833,
[LCL#2104]; master Alexander McBride, from Glasgow to
Montreal in March 1845. [EEC#211159]; from Glasgow *with
passengers* bound for Montreal on 25 July 1845,
[SG#14/1418]

EUXINE, Captain Nicol, from Glasgow to Newfoundland on 17
September 1839, [SG#8/808]; Captain Livingstone, from the
Clyde to New Orleans on 27 November 1850. [EEC#22050];
Captain Watson, from the Clyde to Quebec 14 April 1858,
[CM#21393]

EVELIN, Captain Duggan, from Glasgow *with passengers* bound
for New York on 12 April 1842. [GSP#710]

EXCEL, 600 tons, Captain Sherwood, from Glasgow *with
passengers* bound for New York on 25 April 1843. [GSP#800]

EXPORTER, a 564 ton barque, Captain James Robertson, from Leith
to Quebec on 8 July 1847; from Leith *with passengers* bound
for St John, New Brunswick, on 20 June 1848;from Leith *with
passengers* bound for St John's, New Brunswick, on 1 March
1849; from Leith to St John's, New Brunswick, on 30 June
1849; from Leith *with passengers* bound for St John's, New
Brunswick, on 1 March 1850.
[EEC#21518/21666/21761/21830/21925]

FAIRFIELD, 725 tons, Captain Wilson, from Glasgow to New York on
7 June 1841;from Glasgow *with passengers* bound for New
York on 17 June 1844. [GSP#666/861]

FAIRY, Captain Drummond, from the Clyde to Quebec in May 1858,
[CM#21419]

FAMA, a 131 ton bark, master John Crews, from Greenock *with
passengers* to St Andrews, new brunswick, on 20 march
1830. [GkAd#3435]; Captain Wright, from Greenock *with 84
passengers* bound for Quebec, arrived there on 12 August
1834. [MG]

FAME, Captain Goudy, from the Clyde to Boston on 2 March 1853.
[EEC#22402]

FANNY, Captain McDowell, from Greenock to Newfoundland on 2
November 1838. [SG#7/715]

FANNY, 367 tons, from Alloa to Canada *with 1 passenger* on 15
April 1844. [BPP.35.503]

FANNY, 500 tons, from Glasgow to New Orleans on 28 August 1840, [GSP#689];Captain Sampson, from the Clyde to New York on 11 May 1847. [EEC#21500]

FASIDE, Captain McArthur, from the Clyde to Quebec, arrived there on 29 May 1833, [SG#2/152]; arrived in Quebec from the Clyde on 10 October 1834. [AJ#4532]; Captain Houstoun, from the Clyde to Miramachi April 1858, [CM#21388]

FAVOURITE OF GREENOCK, a 404 ton brig, Captain Burns, from Greenock *with 86 passengers* bound for Quebec on 26 July 1834, arrived there on 26 August 1834, [MG] [SG#3/270]; Captain Greenhorn, from the Clyde to Quebec in July 1837, [CM#18303]; from Glasgow *with 68 passengers* bound for Canada by 4 April 1842, [GSP#712]; from Glasgow to Canada *with 78 passengers* on 5 April 1843; from the Clyde to Montreal 26 August 1843 *with 53 passengers*; from Glasgow to Montreal and Quebec in March 1845; Captain Grant, arrived in Quebec on 14 May 1846 *with 39 passengers* from Glasgow, [MT]; Captain Wyllie, from the Clyde to Montreal on 16 April 1848; from the Clyde to Quebec and Montreal on 24 August 1849; Captain Crawford, from the Clyde to Montreal on 13 April 1850, arrived there on 20 May 1850; from the Clyde to Quebec on 24 August 1850. [BPP.35.503][SG#11/1199] [EEC#20639/21159/ 21645/ 21855/21954/21978/22010]

FAVOURITE, Captain Gribben, from Ayr *with 33 passengers* bound for Quebec, arrived there on 11 July 1834. [MG]

FIDELITY, Captain English, from Leith to Quebec on 31 March 1829. [LCL#1680]

FINGALTON, Captain Craig, from the Clyde to Quebec on 6 July 1850; from the Clyde to Quebec on 10 July 1851. [EEC#21990/22145]

FLORA, Captain Hardie, from Dundee to New York on 20 July 1833. [FH#594]; 230 tons, from Dundee to Canada *with 57 passengers* on 28 April 1843, [BPP.35.503]

FLORA, a 360 ton brig, master Peter Alexander, from Dundee to New York *with passengers* in April 1843; arrived in New York on 21 June 1843 [DW#115][USNA.M237/52]

FLORA, from Glasgow to New York in March 1847. [EEC#21498]

FLORENTIA, Captain Tindale, from the Clyde to New York on 1 June 1850. [EEC#21975]

FLOYD, a 230 to US brig, master E. Denett, from Greenock *with passengers* bound for New York in March 1830. [GkAd#3428]

FORTH, master Robert Hunter, from Greenock *with passengers* to St John, New Brunswick, in March 1830, [GkAd#3428]; from Glasgow to St John's, New Brunswick, in September 1832. [CM#17337]

FORTUNA, Captain Longmuir, from Aberdeen to New York on 12 July 1842. [LCL#1/89]

FOURTEEN, Captain Wilson, from the Clyde to Quebec on 20 May 1850. [EEC#21969]

FRANCIS, a 350 ton American ship, master Norman Peck, from Greenock *with passengers* to New York 2 April 1831, [GkAd#3631]; master Joseph Griffiths, from Greenock *with passengers* bound for New York on 23 July 1831, [PA#101]; from Greenock *with passengers* to New York 12 November 1831, [GkAd#3694]; from Greenock *with passengers* bound for New York on 6 October 1833, [SG#2/182]; from Greenock *with 131 passengers* bound for New York in August 1836. [AJ#4624]

FRANCES DE PAU, 600 tons, Captain Forbes, from Glasgow *with passengers* bound for New York on 10 August 1842. [GSP#765]

FRANCONIA, Captain Boyle, from Glasgow to New York on 1 May 1850. Arrived *with passengers* 29 May 1850 [EEC#21961]

FRANKLAND, 793 tons, from Greenock *with passengers* bound for New York on 5 June 1842. [GSP#718]

FRASERBURGH, from the Clyde to California in September 1854. [EEC#22629]

FREE TRADER, Captain Wade, from the Clyde to Montreal on 4 July 1850. [EEC#21988]

FRIENDSHIP, Captain McCallum, from the Clyde to Boston on 29 May 1851, [EEC#22127]

FUNCHAL, Captain Clift, from Greenock *with 3 passengers* bound for Newfoundland on 16 August 1839. [SG#8/796]

GANGES, Captain Mitchell, from Greenock to Restigouche on 5 May 1839. [SG#8/766]

GARLAND, Captain Martin, from the Clyde to Philadelphia on 11 July 1850. [EEC#21992]

GARRICK, 1004 tons, Captain Palmer, from Glasgow *with passengers* bound for New York on 13 August 1841; Captain Trask, from Glasgow *with passengers* bound for New York on 11 August 1844. [GSP#676/867]

GARTSHERRIE, Captain Ritchie, from the Clyde to Pictou on 14 April 1850, arrived there on 12 May 1850. [EEC#21954/21976]

GAZELLE, from the Clyde bound for Newfoundland in June 1843. [EEC#20629]

GEM, 180 tons, Captain Peter Robb, from Leith *with passengers* bound for Quebec and Montreal in June 1842. [EEC#20360]

GENERAL, 500 tons, from Glasgow to New York on 9 March 1841. [GSP#655]

GENERAL GOLDIE, a schooner, from Dumfries *with 10 passengers* bound for Quebec, arrived there on 14 September 1817. [MG]

GENERAL GRAHAM, 429 tons, Captain Craigie, from Leith to Miramachi on 3 April 1829, [LCL#1681]; Captain Jamieson from Alloa to Miramachi 4 April 1840, [LCL]; from Alloa to Canada *with 3 passengers* on 4 August 1843, [BPP.35.503]

GENERAL VEZIE, a 443 ton American ship, Captain Connillard, from Glasgow *with passengers* bound for New Orleans on 10 October 1842; from Glasgow *with passengers* bound for New Orleans in March 1843. [GSP#773/779]

GENERAL WASHINGTON, a 450 ton American ship, Captain Marbury, from Glasgow *with passengers* bound for Baltimore and Virginia on 25 March 1843. [GSP#779/795]

GENESEE, a 460 ton American ship, from Glasgow *with passengers* bound for New York in July 1841. [GSP#673]

GENTOO, 435 tons, Captain Hellis, from Glasgow to New York on 4 May 1840. [GSP#673]

GEORGE, Captain Brown, from Leith *with 90 passengers* bound for Montreal on 10 April 1830. [LCL#1787]; from Leith to Quebec on 17 September 1830. [LCL#1833]

GEORGE, from Glasgow to Montreal on 10 April 1841, [GSP#659]

GEORGE, 462 tons, Captain Thomson, from Glasgow *with passengers* bound for New Orleans on 8 October 1842. [GSP#773]

GEORGE OF DUNDEE, 676 tons, master William Rae, from Leith *with passengers* bound for Savannah in October 1840. [S#24/2163]

GEORGE OF DUNDEE, 1100 tons, from Glasgow *with passengers* bound for New York on 5 August 1842, [GSP#825]; *with passengers* bound for Quebec in July 1843. [EEC#20635][LCL#3179]

GEORGE, 676 tons, Captain Francis Hanley, from Glasgow *with passengers* bound for New York on 25 July 1842. [GSP#825]; from Dundee to Pictou, Quebec and Montreal *with 56 passengers* on 10 June 1843, via Wick *with 245 passengers* bound for Canada on 1 July 1843. [BPP.35.503][DW#118]

GEORGE, from Loch Laxford *with 307 passengers* bound for Pictou, Nova Scotia, in 1843.

GEORGE, 476 tons, from Leith to Quebec in April 1848; Captain Jones, from Leith to Quebec on 8 April 1853; from Leith to Quebec 15 April 1854. [EEC#21641/22417][LCL#4186/4292]

GEORGE, Captain Parkinson, from the Clyde via Oban bound for Montreal on 20 June 1850; Captain Hogg, from the Clyde to Montreal on 23 April 1851. [EEC#21984/22112]

GEORGE, a barque, to Quebec in August 1850. [EEC#22012]

GEORGE BARCLAY, from Greenock *with 47 passengers* bound for Pictou on 24 July 1834, [SG#3/270]; arrived in Pictou on 26 August 1834 *with 47 passengers* from Greenock. [PANS#282/118]

GEORGE CANNING OF DUNDEE, Captain Kidd, from Dundee via Wick to St John's, New Brunswick, on30 March 1846. [DPCA#2333]

GEORGE GORDON, a brig, Captain Thomas King, from Leith bound for St John, New Brunswick, on 25 July 1831; from Grangemouth bound for St John's, New Brunswick, in April 1843. [EEC#18668/20599]

GEORGE MCLEOD, Captain Dickson, from Greenock to Halifax, Nova Scotia, on 10 September 1839. [SG#8/803]

GEORGE SKOLFIELD, 420 tons, Captain Skolfield, from Glasgow *with passengers* bound for Boston on 28 March 1844. [GSP#841]

GEORGE WASHINGTON, a 700 ton American ship, from Glasgow *with passengers* bound for New York on 25 July 1840; Captain Burrens, from Glasgow to New York on 23 March 1841; from Glasgow *with passengers* bound for New York on 25 July 1841; Captain Allan, from Glasgow *with passengers* bound for New York on 20 July 1844. [GSP#653/657/673/685/866]; Captain Thomas Snow, from Glasgow *with passengers* bound for New York on 28 July 1848, [SG#17/1737]

GEORGES, Captain Ogilvy, from Greenock to Quebec, abandoned at sea during 1833. [SG#2/159]

GEORGIA, Captain Allan, arrived in New York on 27 March 1851 from the Clyde, [EEC#22108]

GEORGINA, Captain Stewart, from Greenock to Montreal on 8 May 1839, [SG#8/766]

GERMANIA, Captain Armstrong, from the Clyde to Philadelphia on 3 May 1851. [EEC#22117]

GERARD, an American ship of 345 tons, Captain Rairden, from Glasgow *with passengers* to New Orleans 26 January 1842. [GH#4067]

GILMOUR, Captain McArthur, from Greenock to Quebec on 4 April 1839; from Glasgow to Quebec on 13 August 1839. [SG#8/757; 8/793]; Captain drysdale, from Leith to St John's 2 March 1843. [LCL#3131]

GIMLE, Captain Juell, from the Clyde to New York on 15 June 1851; from the Clyde to New York on 30 May 1855.
[EEC#22135/21972]

GIPSY, from Tobermory, Mull, *with 316 passengers* bound for Cape Breton Island in Spring 1832, [CM#17337]; Captain Purdy, from the Clyde to Boston on 11 June 1849, [EEC#21822]; from the Clyde to Boston on 10 March 1850; Captain McGregor, from the Clyde to Newfoundland on 26 June 1850; from the Clyde to Newfoundland on 28 August 1850; from the Clyde to Newfoundland on 7 December 1850; from the Clyde to Newfoundland on 19 April 1851.
[EEC#21939/21985/22012/22054/22111]

GIRARD, Captain Rich, from Glasgow to New Orleans on 16 February 1834. [SG#2/222]

GLADIATOR, from the Clyde to Montreal during August 1853.
[EEC#22487]

GLAMIS CASTLE, a 342 ton barque, master Alexander Barclay, from Dundee to New York *with passengers* on 20 December 1843, [DW#150]; Captain Duncan, from Dundee to New York in November 1845, [NW#5/250]; from Dundee to New York in February 1846. [EEC#21313]

GLANCE, a schooner, Captain J. Hardie, from Leith to Montreal on 28 March 1845; from the Clyde to New York in May 1855.
[EEC#21158/22749]

GLASGOW, a 450 ton US ship, master Norman Peck, from Greenock *with passengers* to New York in February 1832.
[GkAd#3694]

GLASGOW, a 1962 ton steamship, from Glasgow to Quebec in June 1840; Captain Ritchie, from the Clyde to St John's, New Brunswick, on 19 July 1849; Captain Ritchie, from the Clyde to Quebec on 1 April 1850; master Robert Craig, from Glasgow *with passengers* bound for New York on 23 February 1853, on 23 April 1853, on 18 June 1853, on 10 August 1853, on 6 October 1853, on 1 December 1853, on 14 February 1854, on 11 April 1854, and on 1 June 1854.
[EEC#20075/21838/21850/21948/22379/22391/22402/22410/2 2427/224821/22533/22547/22593]

GLASGOW, 600 tons, Captain Lambert, from Glasgow *with passengers* bound for Boston on 24 July 1844. [GSP#866]; Captain Marshall, from the Clyde to Boston on 16 March 1850, arrived there on 9 May 1850; Captain Hadfield, from the Clyde to St John's, New Brunswick, on 8 July 1851.
[EEC#21942/21971/22145]

GLASGOW, from Kirkcaldy in April 1853 *with passengers* bound for America, to settle in Wisconsin. [Fife Advertiser#401]

GLASGOW, a 1962 ton steamship, Captain W. Cumming, from Glasgow *with 400 passengers* bound for New York on 11 April 1854; from Glasgow *with passengers* bound for New York on 26 August 1854, also on 21 October 1854, and on 21 November 1854, [EEC#22619/22632/22653]; Captain John Duncan, from Glasgow *with passengers* bound for New York in 1856. [CM#20703][LCL#4292]

GLAUCUS, Captain Banks, from Greenock to St John, Newfoundland, in March 1847. [AJ#5176]

GLEANER, from Greenock to King's Cove, wrecked in May 1833. [SG#2/157]

GLEANER, a 514 ton barque, Captain Thomas Gale, from Campbelltown *with 107 passengers* bound for New York, arrived there on 5 July 1842. [USNA#M237/49]

GLEANER, Captain Duncan, from the Clyde to Quebec on 5 April 1849. [EEC#21793]

GLENCAIRN, Captain Crawford, from the Clyde to Quebec in May 1853; Captain Bulford, from Ayr to St Jhn's, New Brunswick, 13 June 1858. [EEC#22448][CM#21443]

GLENIFFER OF GREENOCK, a 318 ton brig,from Greenock *with 121 passengers* bound for Quebec on 25 June 1834, arrived in Quebec via Gross Isle on 8 August 1834, [MG]; Captain Simpson, from Greenock *with 26 passengers* bound for Quebec on 13 August 1838, [SG#7/699]; Captain MacEwing, from Greenock to New York on 25 February 1839. [EEC#19925][SG#8/746]

GLIDE, Captain Harrison, from the Clyde to Montreal on 10 April 1850. [EEC#21952]

GLOBE, 300 tons, Captain Parker, from Glasgow to St John in March 1841, [GSP#655]

GLOBE, Captain Ritchie, from Leith to Quebec 7 April 1854. [LCL#4290]

GONDOLA, 440 tons, Captain Reund, from Glasgow to New York on 11 April 1841, [GSP#659]

GOOD INTENT, 495 tons, Captain Whitburn, from Glasgow *with passengers* bound for Quebec and Montreal in April 1843. [GSP#779]

GOODWIN, a 800 ton American ship, Captain Davies, from Glasgow to Philadelphia in April 1841; from Glasgow *with passengers* bound for Philadelphia on 16 September 1841. [GSP#657/682]

GORDON CASTLE, Captain Hogg, from Leith to Quebec on 2 August 1829. [LCL#1715]

GORMOR DANS, 700 tons, Captain Neet, from Glasgow *with passengers* bound for Boston on 8 August 1844.[GSP#867]

GOVERNOR BRIGGS, from the Clyde to Philadelphia in May 1854.
[EEC#22595]

GOVERNOR HINCKLEY, a 416 ton American barque, Captain W.
Laing, from Glasgow *with passengers* to New York on 16
September 1849. [EEC#21864][SG#18/1854]

GOVERNOR TROUP, 450 tons, Captain Butman, from Glasgow to
New York on 10 June 1840. [GSP#678]

GRACE DARLING, Captain Boyle, from the Clyde to California on 26
June 1850. [EEC#21985]

GRANGE OF GREENOCK, to Quebec in June 1850. [EEC#21992]

GRANVILLE, Captain Brown, arrived in Boston on 25 April 1850 from
the Clyde. [EEC#21966]

GRATIA, Captain Prowse, from the Clyde to Newfoundland on 5 July
1849; Captain Kewley, from the Clyde to Newfoundland on 12
March 1850, arrived at St John, Newfoundland, on 1 April
1850; from the Clyde to Newfoundland on 2 October 1850.
[S#3531] [EEC#21940/21833/21966/22026]

GREAT BRITAIN, a 694 ton bark, Captain Preal, from Glasgow
passengers bound for New York on 8 August
1844.[GSP#867]

GREAT BRITAIN, a bark, Captain Montgomery, from Glasgow on 7
September 1844 *with 5 passengers,* arrived in Quebec on
18 October 1844. [MT]

GREENOCK, from Loch Laxford *with 417 passengers from Farr
and Tongue, Sutherland,* bound for Canada, arrived in
Quebec on 7 July 1848. [GHF#324][TGSI#45.340]

GULNARE, Captain Dodge, from Lerwick to Boston on 9 April 1849.
[EEC#21798]

GUTHRIE, Captain Will, from Aberdeen to Quebec on 11 April 1850.
[EEC#21955]

HAIDEE, 288 tons, Captain Alexander McBride, from Leith *with
passengers* bound for Quebec and Montreal on 15 July 1841.
[EEC#20230]

HAMILTON, 638 tons, Captain James Dick, from Glasgow *with 263
passengers, mostly farmers* bound for Quebec and
Montreal on 2 June 1842, [FJ#545]; from Glasgow bound for
Quebec *with 263 passengers* on 2 June 1843.
[EEC#20596][BPP.35.503]; from Greenock to New Orleans
with passengers in December 1843. [DW#148]

HAMPTON, Captain Balderson, from Alloa to Quebec 30 March 1840,
[LCL#2828]; Captain Graham, from Glasgow to Quebec in
March 1841, [GSP#655]; from Grangemouth to St John's, New
Brunswick, on 6 March 1849; from Grangemouth to Quebec in
August 1849; from Grangemouth to Quebec on 27 March 1850;

Captain Bogle, from Grangemouth to Quebec 30 March 1858.
[EEC#21782/21853/21946][CM#21381]

HANNAH, a brigantine, master Thomas Wilkie, from Port Glasgow via Cork to New York in 1779. [NAS.AC9/3182]

HANNAH OF DUNDEE, 280 ton brig, Captain David Airth, from Leven *with 4 passengers* bound for Montreal on 28 March 1834. [FJ#60]

HANNAH, Captain James Wallace, from Arbroath to Quebec *with 37 adults and children* in 1854, arrived in June 1854.

HANNAH KERR, Captain Marr, from Troon to New York on 8 March 1849; from Troon to St John's, New Brunswick, on 7 August 1849; from Troon to New York on 13 March 1850.
[EEC#21783/21848/21942]

HANNAH THORNTON, Captain Hovey, from the Clyde to Philadelphia on 21 August 1850; from the Clyde to Philadelphia on 15 December 1850. [EEC#22008/22058]

HARBINGER, a 325 ton barque, master P. Thomson, from Grangemouth to New York in January 1844. [DW#154]

HARLEQUIN, Captain Torrance, from the Clyde to Montreal in April 1858. [CM#21394]

HARMONIA, Captain Churchill, arrived in New York from Glasgow in 1849, [SG#18/1834]; from the Clyde to New York on 16 March 1850; from the Clyde to New York on 13 July 1850; Captain Daggett, from the Clyde to New York on 26 November 1850; from the Clyde to New York on 5 June 1851.
[EEC#21942/21993/22049/22130]

HARMONY, Captain Young, from Leith *with 86 passengers* bound for Quebec on 8 April 1829. [LCL#1682]

HARMONY, Captain McClintock, from the Clyde to Miramachi in August 1840. [EEC#20129]

HARMONY, Captain Anderson, from Troon to Dalhousie, New Brunswick, on 13 April 1848; from Troon to Dalhousie on 10 April 1849; from Troon to Quebec on 6 August 1849; from Troon to Quebec on 10 April 1850.
[EEC#21645/21797/21953/21848]

HARMONY OF IRVINE, to Quebec in September 1849.
[EEC#21870]

HARMONY, Captain McLean, from Ardrossan to Quebec in August 1853. [EEC#22481]

HARPER, from the Broomielaw, Glasgow on 11 April 1842 *with passengers from Paisley and Renfrewshire* bound for Quebec, arrived there on 9 June 1842. [EEC#20386]

HARPER, a 345 ton barque, Captain Murphy, from Leith *with passengers* bound for Quebec and Montreal on 2 May 1844. [EEC#21023][LCL#3256]

HARRIET, Captain Alexander, from Aberdeen to Sydney, Cape Breton, on 27 April 1841. [LCL#3461]

HARRIET, Captain Berry, from the Clyde to New York on 9 May 1851. [EEC#22119]

HARRIET ROCKWELL, a 523 ton American ship, Captain Briard, from Glasgow *with passengers* bound for City Point, Virginia, on 12 July 1842. [GSP#825]

HARRISON CHILTON, Captain Verrill, from the Clyde to Quebec on 23 May 1851, [EEC#22125]

HARVEST HOME, Captain Goodwin, from Ardrossan to Quebec 19 April 1858, [CM#21396]

HAZARD, Captain Kewley, from the Clyde to Newfoundland on 5 March 1853. [EEC#22404]

HEADLEYS, master John Morris, from Cromarty to Quebec *with 230 passengers*, mainly from Banff and Moray, on 24 March 1832. [AJ#4398]

HEBE, a 237 ton brig, Captain Hutton, from Leith *with 51 passengers* to Quebec/Montreal 2 June 1835, [LCL#2323]; Captain Thomson, from Leith to Quebec and Montreal on 9 April 1841, [LCL#3455]; from Leith *with passengers* bound for Montreal in April 1846. [EEC#21301]

HEBRON OF BOSTON, Captain Hood, from Glasgow to Boston on 23 June 1843. [SG#11/1199]

HECTOR, 247 tons, from Glasgow to Canada *with 92 passengers* on 12 July 1843; from Glasgow to Canada *with 138 passengers* on 21 May 1844. [BPP.35.503]

HECTOR, Captain Moir, from Dundee to Montreal on 25 April 1848. [EEC#21651]

HELEN, Captain Taylor, from the Clyde to St John, New Brunswick, on 31 May 1849; from the Clyde to St Joh's, New Brunswick, on 1 August 1849; Captain Sutherland, from the Clyde to Newfoundland on 5 September 1849; Captain Taylor, from the Clyde to Newfoundland on 24 June 1850; Captain Hoggart, from the Clyde to Newfoundland on 3 October 1850; Captain Taylor, from the Clyde to Newfoundland on 18 June 1851; Captain Clark, from the Clyde to Newfoundland on 5 March 1853. [EEC#21817/21844 /21859 /21985/22026/22136/22404]

HELEN, Captain Ritchie, from Aberdeen to Quebec 29 April 1858, [CM#21404]

HELEN OF MONTROSE, Captain Johnston, from Montrose to Quebec on 12 April 1849; from Montrose to Quebec on 3 August 1849; from Montrose to Quebec on 5 April 1850, arrived there on 14 May 1850; from Montrose to Quebec on 9 July 1850; from Montrose *with passengers* bound for Quebec

in April 1853; from Montrose to Quebec 4 April 1854.
[EEC#21798/21845/21951/21976/21992]
[LCL#4186/4289]

HELEN DOUGLAS, a brig, master Alexander Forrest, from Annan, Dumfries-shire, to Richibucto, New Brunswick, in 1830. [DCr: 2.3.1830]

HELEN MARIA, from Glasgow to Philadelphia in February 1853. [EEC#22409]

HELEN THOMSON, Captain Gray, from the Clyde to St Johns on 31 August 1849, [EEC#21858]; from Troon to Philadelphia on 12 March 1850; Captain Brown, from Troon *with 34 passengers* bound for Quebec, shipwrecked on the Bird Islands on 18 May 1854 but passengers saved. [S#3151/3531][EEC#21940/22592]

HELENA, Captain King, from Greenock to Halifax, Nova Scotia, on 26 August 1839, [SG#8/798]

HELLENA, Captain Laird, from Greenock to Newfoundland on 24 August 1839, [SG#8/798]

HENBURY, from Montrose to Canada in April 1851, [EEC#22118]

HENRIETTA MARY, 847 tons, Captain Gortley, from Glasgow *with passengers* bound for Quebec and Montreal on 5 April 1844. [GSP#848]

HENRY, Captain Ross, from Dundee to Quebec on 4 April 1840. [LCL]

HENRY, a 412 ton American ship, Captain Pierce, from Glasgow *with passengers* bound for New Orleans on 27 April 1843. [GSP#796]

HENRY, 315 tons, Captain Johnston, from Leith to Halifax, NS, in March 1843. [LCL#3136]

HENRY, a brig, Captain Anderson, from Glasgow *with 198 passengers* bound for Montreal, arrived there on 18 July 1834. [MG]

HENRY OF MONTROSE, Captain Bowers, from Montrose to Quebec on 12 April 1849; from Montrose to Quebec on 7 August 1849; Captain Forbes, from Montrose to Quebec on 5 April 1850; from Montrose to Quebec on 1 August 1850; from Montrose to Quebec on 3 April 1851; from Montrose to Quebec in April 1853; from Montrose to Quebec 3 April 1854; from Montrose to Quebec 6 August 1854. [LCL#3976/4186/4289/4324] [EEC#21798/21848/21951/22002/22104]

HENRY, Captain Young, from Ardrossan to Quebec on 3 August 1849, [EEC#21846]

HENRY AND WILLIAM, a brig, arrived in Sydney, Cape Breton Island, *with 44 passengers* from Stornaway in 1837. [PANS#338/72; 252/127]

HENRY HOLLAND, a brig, from the Clyde to St John, New Brunswick, in March 1853. [EEC#22408]

HENRY HOOD, from the Clyde to Quebec in June 1847; from the Clyde to Bathurst on 4 May 1848; Captain McArthur, from the Clyde to Bathurst on 7 April 1849; from the Clyde to Bathurst on 14 July 1849; from the Clyde to Bathurst on 22 April 1850; from the Clyde to Bathurst on 11 April 1851; from the Clyde to the Bay of Chaleur in September 1854.[EEC#21520/21653 /21795 /21837 /21951/21996/22108 /22645]

HENRY LEEDS, a 350 ton American ship, Captain Robert Marshall, from Glasgow *with passengers* bound for New York on 5 August 1840; Captain Mosey, from Glasgow *with passengers* bound for New York on 5 August 1842. [GSP#685/826]

HENRY NESMITH, Captain Butler, from the Clyde to New York on 4 July 1851, [EEC#22144]

HENRY PORCHER, Captain Greig, from Grangemouth to Quebec on 1 July 1847; arrived in Quebec from Greenock in 1849; from Grangemouth to Quebec on 27 March 1850; from Alloa to Quebec on 2 August 1850; from Grangemouth to Quebec 1 April 1851. [LCL#3974]
[EEC#21523/21947/22002][SG#18/1836]

HENRY PRATT, 580 tons, Captain Fairfowl, from Glasgow *with passengers* bound for New York on 24 April 1843. [GSP#800]

HENRY WILLARD, from Glasgow to New York in July 1843. [EEC#20640]

HERALD, Captain Goldie, from Dundee to Savannah on 25 March 1830. [PA#34]; arrived in Charleston, South Carolina, on 18 May 1834 from Dundee, [AJ#4512]; arrived in Savannah on 30 May 1834 from Aberdeen; Captain Clark, arrived in Savannah on 10 June 1837 from Aberdeen. [AJ#4514/4671]

HERALD, 911 tons, Captain Auld, from Glasgow *with passengers* to New York on 17 May 1849; from the Clyde to New York on 15 June 1850; from the Clyde to New York on 8 November 1850; from the Clyde to New York on 22 May 1851,[SG#18/1812] [EEC#21811/21981/22042/22126]

HERALD, Captain Jones, from the Clyde to Montreal on 10 May 1851.[EEC#22120]

HERCULEAN, Captain Chase, from the Clyde to Boston on 17 July 1849, [EEC#21838]

HERCULES, a 400 ton barque, Captain Duncan Walker, from Aberdeen *with 90 passengers* to Quebec in 1834. [FAO#113]; from Aberdeen *with 121 passengers* bound for Quebec on 26 July 1834, [AJ#4516]; a barque, arrived in Sydney, Cape Breton Island, *with 70 passengers* from Stornaway in 1837, [PANS#338/72; 252/127]; Captain Walker,

from Aberdeen *with 38 passengers* bound for Quebec on 27
May 1837, and by 27 July 1837 arrived at Quebec,
[AJ#4664/4678]; Captain George Davidson, from Aberdeen to
Restigouche on 6 April 1838; from Aberdeen *with
passengers* bound for Quebec from Aberdeen on 25 April
1839; to Quebec on 20 August 1839; from Aberdeen to Quebec
on 21 May 1840, [AJ#4709/4762/4780/4819]; Captain Palmer,
from the Clyde to St John, New Brunswick, on 2 October 1850.
[EEC#22026]

HERMANN, 420 tons, Captain Alleyn, from Glasgow *with
passengers* bound for Baltimore on 28 March 1844.
[GSP#841]

HERMITAGE, 500 tons, an American ship, Captain French, from
Glasgow *with passengers* bound for New York on 20 July
1838. [SG#7/681]

HERO, a 321 ton brig, from Greenock *with 157 passengers* bound
for Pictou, Nova Scotia, in 1829; Captain Potter, from Greenock
with passengers to Charleston, South Carolina, in February
1830. [GkAd#1830]

HERO, Captain Taylor, from the Clyde to Quebec in August 1837.
[CM#18303]

HEROINE OF ABERDEEN, 550 tons, Captain Duncan Walker,
arrived in Quebec on 9 May 1838 from Aberdeen; from
Aberdeen *with passengers* bound for Quebec on 28 July
1838; from Aberdeen *with passengers* bound for Quebec on
16 August 1839; from Aberdeen *with passengers* bound for
Quebec on 10 April 1840; from Stornaway *with 281
passengers from Skye* bound for Prince Edward Island,
arrived there on 25 September 1840.
[AJ#4718/4723/4779/4811/4842] [PAPEI]; 387 tons, from
Aberdeen to Canada *with 43 passengers* on 6 April 1843,
[BPP.35.503]; 400 tons, master Duncan Walker, from Dundee
to Quebec *with passengers* in August 1843, [DW#130]; 400
tons, Captain Duncan Walker, from Aberdeen *with 69
passengers* bound for Quebec on 28 May 1845, arrived there
14 July 1845. [FAO#77]; from Aberdeen *with passengers*
bound for Quebec on 27 June 1846; from Aberdeen *with
passengers* bound for Quebec on 27 May 1847; Captain
Walker, from Dundee to Quebec on 18 August 1849;from
Aberdeen to Quebec on 11 April 1850; from Dundee to Quebec
on 16 August 1850; from Aberdeen to Quebec on 16 April
1851, arrived there on 26 May 1851. [AJ#5132/5184/5397]
[EEC#21853/21955/22007/22110]

HIBERNIA, Captain Russell, from Greenock to Chaleur Bay on 25
July 1838; from Port Glasgow to Restigouche on 15 April 1839;

from Greenock to Chaleur Bay on 21 August 1839; Captain
Park, from the Clyde to Dalhousie, New Brunswick, on 24 July
1845. [SG#7/685; 8/761; 8/798; 14/1423]

HIBERNIA, 540 tons, Captain Cobb, from Glasgow to New York on
13 June 1840. [GSP#678]

HIBERNIA, 850 tons, Captain Bunting, from Glasgow *with*
passengers bound for New York on 1 May 1843. [GSP#800]

HIBERNIA, Captain Laird, from the Clyde to Quebec on 1 May 1849;
Captain Hyland, from the Clyde to Quebec on 9 April 1850,
sunk on Green Bank on 10 May 1850.
[EEC#21804/21952/21979]

HIBERNIA, Captain English, arrived in St John's, New Brunswick, on
28 April 1849 from Glasgow. [EEC#21810]

HIGHLANDER OF LEITH, a 300 ton brig, master John Mitchell, from
Leith *with 41 passengers* bound for Quebec and Montreal in
April 1833, arrived in Halifax on 11 June 1833 *with 41*
passengers,[LCL#2105] [PANS#282/81]; arrived in Bathurst
on 26 May 1834 from Leith via Halifax, [AJ#4515]; from Leith
with 53 passengers bound for Quebec in July 1835.
[FJ#10/137]; arrived at Grosse Island in September 1836 from
Cromarty. [AJ#4629]

HINDOO, 580 tons, Captain Procter, from Glasgow *with*
passengers bound for New York on 18 March 1844.
[GSP#841]

HOME, a 480 ton barque, Captain Walter Greig, from Glasgow *with*
passengers bound for Halifax, Nova Scotia, and Charleston,
South Carolina, on 29 March 1849; from Glasgow *with*
passengers to Montreal and Quebec on 10 August 1849; from
the Clyde to Montreal on 4 March 1850, arrived there on 22
May 1850; from the Clyde to Montreal on 19 March 1850.
[EEC#21790/21849/21936/21978/22097] [SG#18/1798, 1839,
1846]

HOPE, Captain MacFarlane, from Leith to Quebec *with 20*
passengers on 17 May 1830. [LCL#1797]

HOPE, 880 tons, Captain Seull, from Glasgow *with passengers*
bound for New Orleans on 15 July 1842. [GSP#724]; a 515 ton
barque, master William Grange, from Glasgow *with 143*
passengers bound for Pictou on 7 May 1848. [PANS: Micro
RG1#257/99] [PB#111/112]

HORACE, a 281 ton American brig, Captain John White, from
Glasgow *with passengers* bound for New York on 15 June
1839, [SG#8/770, 779]

HORN, Captain Robertson, from Dundee to Quebec 31 March 1840.
[LCL#2828]

HOUND OF GREENOCK, a schooner, Captain Walters, from Greenock bound for St John, New Brunswick, in August 1844. [GSP#870]; from Greenock to St John's, New Brunswick, in June 1849; Captain Roper, from the Clyde to Newfoundland on 4 March 1853. [EEC#21833/22404]

HOWARD, 440 tons, Captain Gray, from Glasgow to New York on 6 April 1841, [GSP#659]

HUDSON, a 900 ton United States Line ship, Captain Page, from Glasgow *with passengers* bound for New York on 26 June 1844; Captain Russel Doane, from Glasgow *with passengers* to New York on 9 July 1849; Captain Simpson, from the Clyde to New York on 21 March 1850; Captain Hatch, from the Clyde to New York on 19 July 1851; Captain Nelson, arrived in New York on 17 March 1853 from Glasgow. [GSP#860][SG#18/1828] [EEC#21834/22099/22150/22415]

HUMAYOON, Captain MacKenzie, from Dundee to California on 12 August 1850. [EEC#22005]

HUMBER, arrived in New Orleans 5 January 1861 from Ardrossan. [S#1747]

HURON, 500 tons, from Glasgow to Boston on 12 February 1842, *"the railroad now open from Boston to Buffalo renders the route by Boston the most expeditious and cheap mode of travel to Upper Canada, New Brunswick and the Western States".* [GH#4071]; Captain Sibbison, from Glasgow to Montreal on 12 June 1842; Captain Payne, from Glasgow *with passengers* bound for New Orleans on 20 July 1844. [GSP#702/719/866]; Captain Bain, from the Clyde to New York on 5 June 1851, [EEC#22130]

HYNDFORD, 511 tons, Captain Stevenson, from Glasgow *with passengers* to New York on 19 June 1849; from the Clyde to New York on 26 April 1850; from the Clyde to New York on 25 September 1850; from the Clyde to New York on 20 June 1851; from the Clyde to Quebec in August 1854.[SG#18/1826] [EEC#21826/21960/22023/22137/22636]

HYPERION, a 700 ton American ship, Captain Perkins, from Glasgow *with passengers* to New York on 10 August 1849. [EEC#21849][SG#18/1840]

ICENI, Captain McLellan, from the Clyde to Newfoundland on 4 August 1849, [EEC#21846]

IDA, from Ardrossan to Quebec in June 1853; Captain Harvey, from Ardrossan to Boston on 13 May 1855. [EEC#21812/22451]

I DARE, from Loch Ryan to the Bay of Chaleur in May 1851. [EEC#22139]

ILLINOIS, 900 tons, Captain English, from Glasgow *with passengers* bound for New York on 16 April 1843. [GSP#800]

INDEPENDENCE, 730 tons, Captain McCappin, from Glasgow *with passengers* bound for Quebec on 24 May 1840; from Glasgow to New York on 23 January 1841; Captain Nye, from Glasgow to New York on 25 May 1841; from Glasgow *with passengers* bound for New Orleans on 27 September 1842; from Glasgow *with passengers* bound for Quebec and Montreal in April 1843; from Glasgow to New york *with passengers* in 1843; from Glasgow *with passengers* bound for Quebec on 19 June 1844. [GSP#641/666/676/771/779/860][DW#121]

INDIANA, from Leith to Quebec in September 1840. [AJ#4842]

INDIANA, a 300 ton barque, Captain Thomson, from Glasgow *with passengers* to Montreal 25 March 1842. [GH#4071]

INDUS, Captain Nicol, from Greenock to Quebec on 3 April 1839; from Greenock to Quebec on 7 August 1839; Captain Stobo, from Glasgow to Pictou, Nova Scotia, on 1 October 1839. [SG#8/757; 8/793; 8/808]; Captain Roberts, from the Clyde to Quebec on 8 April 1851, [EEC#22106]

INDUSTRY, 450 tons, from Leith *with passengers* bound for Pictou and Quebec on 24 June 1831. [EEC#18660]; a barque from Inverness *with passengers* arrived in Pictou in September 1831. [CP:17 September 1831]

INDUSTRY, a brig, from Dundee *with passengers* bound for Quebec in June 1832. [CM#17314]

INDUSTRY, Captain Thoms, arrived in Halifax in May 1833. [FH#593]

INEZ, from Greenock *with 91 passengers* bound for New York on 14 July 1834. [SG#3/270]

INNES, Captain Ovenstone, from Leith *with 12 passengers* to Quebec/Montreal 11 April 1835. [LCL#2302]

INTEGRITY, Captain Joplin, from the Clyde to Miramachi on 30 April 1851. [EEC#22115]

IONTHE, Captain McAllister, from the Clyde to Boston on 15 June 1848. [EEC#21670]

IOWA, Captain Blake, from the Clyde to New York on 9 November 1850. [EEC#22042]

IRENE, Captain F. A. Meyer, from Aberdeen to New York on 26 October 1840. [AJ#4842]

IRIS, from the Clyde via Islay to Quebec on 20 May 1833, [SG#2/144]

IRONSIDES, a 300 ton ironship, from Glasgow to Texas on 5 September 1840. [GSP#690]

IRVINE, 300 tons, Captain Madgurck, from Glasgow *with passengers* bound for New York on 1 April 1844. [GSP#841]

ISAAC ALLERTON, 600 tons, Captain Torrey, from Glasgow *with passengers* bound for New Orleans on 30 July 1844. [GSP#866]

ISAAC NEWTON, Captain Bush, from the Clyde to New Orleans on 13 February 1850. [EEC#21938]

ISABELLA, from Dundee *with passengers* bound for Quebec in April 1830. [DA,8.4.1830]; Captain Crawford, from Dundee to Quebec on 27 April 1850. [LCL#3880]

ISABELLA, a 376 ton barque, Captain Morris, from Greenock *with passengers* to Pictou in March 1830, [GkAd#3432]; master R. Dunlop, from Greenock *with passengers* to St John, New Brunswick, in March 1831, [GkAd#3626]; from Greenock *with 10 passengers* bound for Nova Scotia, landed at Halifax in April 1832, [TN:26.4.1832]; from Greenock *with 21 passengers* bound for Canada in April 1833. [Times#15146]; arrived in Pictou, Nova Scotia, in Spring 1837 *with 190 passengers* from Greenock, and in the Fall 1837 *with 24 passengers* from Greenock, [PANS#252/127; 338/72]; arrived in Sydney, Cape Breton Island, in January 1838 *with 24 passengers* from Greenock, [PANS.Financial Mss., Passenger Money]; Captain William Auld, from Greenock *with 2 passengers* bound to Pictou on 26 July 1838, [SG#7/685-716]; arrived in Pictou on 29 August 1838 *with 37 passengers* from Greenock, [PANS#253/1]; from Port Glasgow *with 118 passengers* bound for Pictou on 12 April 1839; from Greenock to Pictou on 26 July 1839, [SG#8/761, 786]; arrived in Pictou *with 118 passengers* from Greenock in 1839; arrived in Pictou *with 37 passengers* from Greenock in May 1840; arrived in Pictou *with passengers* from Greenock in August 1840; Captain A. Thomas, bound from Glasgow to Pictou *with 54 passengers* on 1 April 1842, ship lost in ice off Cape North, Cape Breton Island, passengers saved and landed in Pictou 11 May 1842.[LCL#1/85]

ISABELLA, Captain Just, from Dundee to Quebec 30 March 1840. [LCL#2828]

ISABELLA OF IRVINE, a brig, Captain Miller, from Troon *with 100 passengers, mainly Ayrshire farmers* bound for Quebec and Montreal in April 1833. [Times#15146]; arrived in Sydney, Cape Breton Island, *with 121 passengers* from Greenock in 1837. [PANS#338/72; 252/127]

ISABELLA, a barque, Captain A. Thomas, from Glasgow on 1 April 1842 *with 54 passengers* bound for Pictou, Nova Scotia, wrecked off Cape North, Cape Breton Island, on 11 May 1842, passengers saved. [EEC#20378][GSP#712]

ISABELLA SIMPSON OF KIRKCALDY, 539 tons, Captain John Bell, from Leith to Miramachi on 1 April 1829, [LCL#1680]; from Leith to Miramachi on 26 July 1829, [LCL#1713]; from Leith to Miramachi on 7 April 1830, [LCL#1786]; from Kirkcaldy **with 37 passengers and others** who embarked at Cromarty, bound for Quebec on 25 March 1834, wrecked on Cape Chat, St Lawrence River, on 15 May 1834, all passengers saved and taken to Quebec. [FJ#58/88][AJ#4513]

ISABELLA STEWART, Captain Hay, from the Clyde to Boston on 24 May 1849. [EEC#21814]

ISLAY, from Isle of Lewis **with 68 passengers** bound for Canada in 1851. [GHF#325]

ISLE OF FRANCE, a barque, from the Clyde to America in July 1854. [EEC#22621]

JACK TAR, Captain McGregor, from Aberdeen to Quebec on 22 June 1834. [AJ#4511]

JAMAICA, master James Heron, arrived in New Orleans on 19 January 1829 **with 3 passengers** from Port Glasgow. [USNA]

JAMAICA, a 356 ton barque, Captain Thomas Martin, from Glasgow **with passengers** bound for Quebec and Montreal on 28 August 1839, [SG#8/795]; Captain Henry, from the Clyde to Quebec and Montreal on 6 July 1845, [SG#14/1418]; from Greenock **with 200 pasengers from Tiree** bound for Quebec on 11 June 1847. [GHF#326][Argyll Estate Papers #1522, Inveraray Castle][EEC#21514][AJ#5188]; from the Clyde to Quebec on 12 June 1849; from the Clyde bound for Quebec on 20 July 1850; from the Clyde to Quebec and Montreal on 27 June 1851, [EEC#21823/21995/22141]

JAMES, Captain Dunlop, from Irvine to Quebec in May 1840. [EEC#20056]

JAMES, Captain Cooper, from Dundee to Quebec on 10 April 1849. [EEC#21796]

JAMES, Captain Feivouz, from the Clyde to Boston on 6 August 1849, [EEC#21846]

JAMES, Captain Hole, from the Clyde to Newfoundland on 6 September 1850; from the Clyde to Newfoundland in December 1854. [EEC#22015/22682]

JAMES CAMPBELL, a 326 ton bark, from Glasgow **with 5 passengers** bound for Canada by 4 April 1842, [GSP#712]; from Glasgow to Montreal in March 1845. [EEC#21159]; Captain Miller, from Glasgow on 29 March 1846 **with 4 passengers** bound for Quebec, landed there on 3 May 1846, [QG][MT]

JAMES CASKIE, Captain Devine, from the Clyde to Quebec in April 1858, [CM#21399]

JAMES DEAN, from Glasgow *with 29 passengers* bound for
Canada by 4 April 1842. [GSP#712]

JAMES H.SHEPHERD, 685 tons, Captain Redman, from Glasgow to
Boston in March 1841, [GSP#655]

JAMES MORAN, 600 tons, Captain D. Ferguson, from Glasgow *with
passengers* bound for New York on 16 April 1844. [GSP#850]

JAMES REDDIN, Captain Roddick, from Annan to Quebec on 25
April 1856; from Annan to Quebec 25 May 1858.
[CM#20778/21426]

JAMES SHEPHERD, 450 tons, from Glasgow to Boston in March
1841. [GSP#654]

JANE, a barque, master W. Holmes, from Greenock to New Orleans in
March 1830, [GkAd#3431]; master David Ritchie, from
Greenock to New Orleans on 4 March 1834, [SG#2/225];
arrived in New Orleans on 5 November 1836 *with 80
passengers* from Greenock. [USNA.M259/114]

JANE, Captain McQuien, from Greenock *with 91 passengers* bound
for New York on 8 June 1839, [SG#8/777]

JANE OF THE CLYDE, a barque, Captain Stobo, from the Clyde to
New York in June 1840. [EEC#20063/20068]

JANE, 750 tons, from Glasgow to New York on 11 March
1841.[GSP#655]

JANE AUGUSTA, 968 tons, Captain Bogart, from Glasgow to New
York on 26 March 1841, [GSP#657]

JANE BOYD, a 387 ton barque, master H. Ganson, from Aberdeen to
Quebec 15 April 1853; from Aberdeen *with emigrants* bound
for Quebec 12 April 1854; arrived in Quebec during May 1854;
Captain Mann, from Aberdeen to Quebec 15 August 1854.
[LCL#4187/4292/4327][AJ#5562]

JANE BROWN, 282 ton barque, master John Wyllie, from Glasgow
with 11 passengers bound for Canada by 4 April 1842,
[GSP#712][GH]; from Glasgow to Montreal and Quebec in
March 1845; Captain Mathew Wallace, from Glasgow *with
passengers* bound for Montreal on 28 July 1845,
[SG#14/1418,1422]; Captain Alexander Leitch, from Glasgow
with passengers bound for Montreal in 1849, [SG#18/1808];
Captain Leitch, from the Clyde to Montreal on 24 August 1850;
from the Clyde to Montreal on 18 July 1851.
[EEC#21159/22010/22150]

JANE CHRISTIE, Captain Scott, from Leith *with 40 passengers*
bound for Quebec and Montreal on 6 April 1837. [LCL#2516]

JANE COCHRANE, from Troon to Quebec April 1858. [CM#21386]

JANE DUFF, Captain Stevenson, from the Clyde to Newfoundland on
10 September 1849; from the Clyde to Newfoundland on 15

April 1850, arrived there on 11 May 1850.
[EEC#21861/21950/21954/21971]

JANE DUFFIE, 382 tons, Captain McDonell, from Glasgow to Canada *with 257 passengers* on 2 May 1843, [BPP.35.503]; arrived in Quebec in June 1843 from the Clyde. [EEC#20631]

JANE GLASSIN, Captain Lawrence, from Leith to Quebec 13 April 1858. [CM#21386]

JANE HADDOW, 340 ton brig, master John Hamilton, from Greenock *with passengers* to New York in February 1830, [GkAd#1830]; from Greenock *with passengers* to New York in December 1831, [GkAd#3706]; from Greenock to New York on 20 February 1839, [SG#8/745]

JANE KEY, a brig, from Cromarty and Thurso in June 1833 *with 106 passengers* for Pictou and *51 passengers* for Quebec. [CP:23.7.1833]

JANE MELRAIN, 300 tons, from Glasgow to Quebec in April 1841, [GSP#657]

JANET, from Stornaway *with passengers* bound for Port Hawkesbury, Cape Breton Island, in 1834. [TGSI#55.344]

JANET, Captain McBride, from Greenock to Dalhousie on 7 August 1839, [SG#8/793]

JANET, Captain Melville, arrived in St John, New Brunswick, in April 1840 from the Clyde. [EEC#20051]

JANET, 519 tons, Captain David Fraser, from Glasgow *with passengers* bound for New York on 10 May 1842. [GSP#714]

JANET, a 319 ton brigantine, master Alexander Brown, from Glasgow to New York *with passengers* in March 1843. [DW#112]

JANET, Captain McIntosh, from Grangemouth to St John's, New Brunswick, on 7 March 1849; from the Clyde to Quebec on 11 July 1849; from the Clyde to Halifax and Pictou on 6 April 1850. [EEC#21782/21835/21951]

JANET OF PORT GLASGOW, to Boston in July 1850. [EEC#22007]

JANET, Captain Ballingall, arrived in Boston on 11 April 1851 from the Clyde, [EEC#22114]

JANET, 238 tons, Captain Craigie, from Leith *with 14 passengers* bound for Montreal 4 April 1843; Captain Kidd, from Leith to Montreal 3 April 1854. [LCL#3141/4289]

JANET IZAT, from Greenock via Tobermory, Mull, *with 210 passengers* bound for Port Hawkesby, Cape Breton, and Quebec on 17 July 1834. [SG#3/270][TGSI.LV.343]

JANSEN, a 300 ton brig, from Leith to California 1 March 1849. [EEC#21772]

JEAN, Captain Jack, from Leith to Quebec on 7 April 1830. [LCL#1786]

JEAN BAPTISTE, Captain Gellatly, from Greenock to Quebec on 3 April 1839, [SG#8/757]

JEAN HADDOW, a 345 ton brig, master Robert Suttie, from Greenock *with passengers* bound for New York on 12 May 1840. [S#24/2119]

JEAN HASTIE, a 500 ton barque, from Greenock *with 6 passengers* bound for Nova Scotia, arrived in Halifax on 15 April 1833; from Greenock 19 June 1833 *with 8 passengers* bound for Nova Scotia, landed at Halifax on 22 July 1833; from Greenock in April 1834 *with 13 passengers* bound for Nova Scotia, arrived at Halifax in May 1834; from Greenock in August 1834 *with 7 passengers* bound for Nova Scotia, arrived in Halifax in October 1834. [TN#8.5.1834; 2.10.1834] [PANS#2882/81]; 280 tons, from Dundee to Montreal *with 18 passengers* on 27 June 1843, via Wick on 4 July 1843 [BPP.35.503][DW#123]

JEAN WILSON, Captain Paton, from Dundee to New York on 10 May 1830. [PA#40]

JEANNIE DEANS, 319 tons, from Glasgow to Canada *with 75 passengers* on 2 May 1843, [BPP.35.503]

JEHIGH, 500 tons, Captain Plummer, from Glasgow to Philadelphia in May 1841. [GSP#662]

JENNY LIND, Captain Power, from the Clyde to Montreal on 28 June 1849, [EEC#21830]

JESSIE, from Tobermory, Mull, *with 313 passengers* bound for Nova Scotia, landed at Sydney, Cape Breton Island, on 10 September 1832. [PANS#282/48]

JESSIE, a 950 ton United States Line ship, Captain Irvine, from Glasgow *with passengers* to Boston and Quebec on 11 July 1849; Captain Isbister, from Ardrossan to Boston in March 1850, arrived there on 13 April 1850. [EEC#21835/21935/21960][SG#18/1833]

JESSIE AMELIA, a 500 ton brig, Captain H. Eccleston, from the Broomielaw, Glasgow, *with passengers* bound for Montreal on 20 June 1844. [GSP#860]

JESSIE ANN, a 172 ton brig, Captain P. Sim, from Leith to Montreal on 2 April 1847. [EEC#21452]

JESSIE GREIG, 220 tons, Captain Greig, from Leith to Montreal in April 1843. [LCL#3140]

JESSIES, Captain Christie, from Leith *with 54 passengers* bound for Montreal on 7 April 1829. [LCL#1682]

JOANNA, 555 tons, Captain Riddoch, from Alloa to St John's, New Brunswick, on 27 February 1841; from Alloa to St John's, New Brunswick, on 16 March 1850, arrived in St John's, New Brunswick, on 12 April 1850 from Alloa; from Leith to St John's,

New Brunswick, in June 1851; from Leith to Quebec in July 1854; Captain Pennie, from Leith to Quebec 13 April 1858; Captain Wyllie, from Leith to Quebec April 1860; Captain Armour, from Leith to Quebec on 9 August 1860. [LCL#418/4915/4953][EEC#21781/21943/22117/22138/23525] [CM#21386]

JOHN, Captain McFarlane, from Leith to Quebec *with 80 passengers* on 2 June 1830. [LCL#1802]

JOHN, Captain Mann, from Leith to Quebec *with 15 passengers* on 9 June 1830. [LCL#1804]

JOHN, a brig, from Greenock on 31 March 1833 *with 3 passengers* bound for Nova Scotia, landed at Halifax on 22 April 1833. [PANS#282/81]

JOHN, Captain Casely from Leith to Montreal 18 April 1857. [LCL#4606]

JOHN AND MARY, Captain Nicholson, from Leith *with 79 passengers* to Quebec on 10 June 1834, arrived there on 12 August 1834. [FJ#76][MG]

JOHN AND ROBERT, from Glasgow to Quebec on 10 May 1840, [GSP#673]; 501 tons, Captain McKechnie, from Glasgow to Montreal on 22 June 1842; from Glasgow *with passengers* bound for Quebec on 8 June 1844. [GSP#860/719]

JOHN BELL, from Glasgow *with passengers* to New York 23 February 1861. [S#1757]

JOHN BUNYAN, from the Clyde to New York in January 1860. [DC#23470]

JOHN CUMMING, 600 tons, Captain Thayer, from Glasgow to Philadelphia in January 1841; from Glasgow to New York on 5 July 1841; from Glasgow to Canada *with 83 passengers* on 16 June 1843, [BPP.35.503]; from Glasgow *with passengers* bound for New York on 16 March 1844. [GSP#647/668/841]

JOHN DUNLOP, 437 tons, Captain Choate, from Glasgow *with passengers* bound for Baltimore on 6 August 1841. [GSP#676]

JOHN GRAY, Captain McDonald, from the Clyde to California on 11 October 1850. [EEC#22031]

JOHN HAMILTON, 942 tons, master Peter Sillars, from Greenock *with passengers* bound for Quebec and Montreal in July 1854. [EEC#22611][AJ#5562]

JOHN HECTOR, Captain Henry, from Aberdeen to the Chesapeake on 23 March 1847, arrived in Norfolk, Virginia, on 3 May 1847. [AJ#5177/5187]

JOHN KERR OF GREENOCK, Captain Taitt, from Glasgow *with 4 passengers* to Miramachi on 9 August 1839, [SG#8/794]; from the Clyde with passengers in May 1844, [GSP#856];

Captain Perkins, from the Clyde to New York on 30 May 1849; Captain Morrison, from the Clyde to St John's, New Brunswick, on 30 March 1850, arrived in St John, Newfoundland, on 11 May 1850 from the Clyde; from the Clyde to Quebec on 8 April 1851. [EEC#21817/21948/21971/22106]

JOHN MCKENZIE, 1600 tons, Captain McKenzie, from the Clyde to New Orleans on 28 November 1850, arrived there on 20 March 1851; Captain Tilley, from Greenock *with passengers* bound for Quebec and Montreal on 8 July 1854, [EEC#22050/22108/22593] [AJ#5553];from the Clyde on 18 May 1857 *with 332 passengers* bound for Quebec, arrived there by 26 June 1857. [Toronto Globe, 2.7.1857]

JOHN MERRICK, Captain Crabtree, arrived in New Orleans 12 December 1860 from the Clyde. [S#1731]

JOHN P. HARWOOD, arrived in New Orleans on 27 April 1850 from the Clyde. [EEC#21971]

JOHN WALKER, from Skye *with 200 passengers* bound for Sydney, Cape Breton, in 1841. [TGSI#55.343]

JOHN WILSON, Captain Copeland, from Dumfries to St John, New Brunswick, on 2 June 1848; from Dumfries to Quebec on 31 March 1849;from Dumfries to St John's, New Brunswick, on 31 July 1849; from Dumfries to St John, New Brunswick, on 22 July 1850; from Dumfries to St John, New Brunswick, on 3 April 1851; Captain Brown, from Dumfries to St John, New Brunswick, 29 March 1858.
[EEC#21666/21792/21844/21998/22105] [CM#21381]

JOHN W. EBRETT, Captain Moffat, from Troon to Boston 24 June 1858. [CM#21451]

JOSEPH GREEN, 353 tons, Captain James Volum, from Peterhead, Cromarty, Scrabster and Lochinver *with 234 passengers, 81 from Caithness, 46 from Sutherland, 86 from Inverness and Ross, and 21 from Aberdeenshire,* bound for Quebec in May 1842. [AJ, 6.4.1842]

JOSEPH PORTER, Captain Reid, from the Clyde to Boston on 17 July 1849, [EEC#21838]

J. P. HARWARD, Captain Andres, from the Clyde to New Orleans on 4 March 1850. [EEC#21936]

JUNIOR, Captain Carter, from the Clyde to New York on 16 May 1851, [EEC#22123]

JUNO, from the Clyde to Quebec on 5 May 1847. [EEC#21497]

JUPITER, Captain Comrie, from Greenock *with 16 passengers* bound for Quebec on 3 April 1834. [SG#3/234]

JUPITER OF GLASGOW, 480 tons, Captain Smith, from Glasgow to Boston on 12 April 1841, [GSP#659]; from Glasgow to Boston on 30 September 1843. [SG#11/1228]

JUSTYN, Captain Scott, from the Clyde to Quebec on 10 June 1851, [EEC#22133]

KATE, from Cromarty to Quebec, arrived there on 9 September 1846. [AJ#5153]

KATHADIN, 1400 tons, Captain Alfred Morse, from the Clyde to New York on 1 May 1849; from Glasgow *with passengers* bound to New York on 21 September 1849. [EEC#21805/21867][SG#18/1856]

KENSINGTON, a 500 ton American ship, Captain Eli Curtis, from Glasgow *with passengers* bound for New York on 23 September 1840. [GSP#691]

KENT OF GREENOCK, master James Gardiner, from Glasgow *with 69 passengers* bound for Montreal by 4 April 1842, [GSP#712][GH#4070]; from Greenock *with 72 passengers* bound for Canada, wrecked on the Seven Islands on 9 May 1842, passengers saved. [EEC#20378][FJ#495]

KESTREL, Captain Corbin, from the Clyde to Newfoundland on 18 April 1849. [EEC#21799]

KILMAURS, a 226 ton barque, Captain Robert Blair, from Glasgow *with 22 passengers* bound for Quebec and Montreal on 20 June 1839, [SG#8/775, 782]

KINCARDINESHIRE, a brig, Captain Morrison, later Captain Gavin, from Leith *with 46 passengers* on 19 June 1839 bound for Quebec and Montreal. [EEC#19895][LCL#2746]

KING, 320 tons, from Glasgow *with passengers* bound for New York on 29 September 1841. [GSP#683]

KING WILLIAM, arrived at Grosse Island on 17 September 1836 from Banff. [AJ#4629]

KINGFISHER, Captain Peace, from Aberdeen to Boston on 24 February 1837. [AJ#4651]

KINGSTAND, 80 tons, Captain McCorran, from Glasgow *with passengers* bound for New York on 6 September 1840. [GSP#691]

KINGSTON OF ABERDEEN, Captain John Cargill, from Aberdeen *with passengers* bound for Quebec on 12 June 1837; from Aberdeen to Quebec on 7 April 1838. [AJ#4661/4709]

LADY CAMPBELL, Captain John Whyte, from Greenock on 29 March 1833 *with 26 passengers from Lanarkshire* bound for St John, New Brunswick, arrived there 21 May 1833; Captain Peter Simpson, from Greenock 22 March 1834 *with 25 passengers from Perthshire, Lanarkshire and Renfrewshire* bound for St John, New Brunswick, arrived there by 17 May 1834. [PANB]

LADY CHARLOTTE GUEST, a clipper, Captain Brewer, from Glasgow *with passengers* bound for St John, New Brunswick, on 10 June 1841. [GSP#667]

LADY COLEBROOKE, a 385 ton barque, from Glasgow *with passengers* bound for Boston in November 1843. [SG.XII/1234]; Captain Peck, from Glasgow to New York on 22 April 1850, arrived *with passengers* 27 May 1850. [EEC#21957]

LADY EMILY, a brig, from Thurso and Loch Laxford *with 150 passengers* bound for Pictou, Nova Scotia, and Quebec in June 1842. [LCL#1/84]

LADY FALKLAND, 672 tons, from Glasgow to Quebec on 24 June 1842. [GSP#721]

LADY GRAY, a brig, master William Gray, from Cromarty and Scrabster *with 240 passengers* bound for Pictou, Nova Scotia, in 1841, arrived there on 16 July 1841. [PB#104/105] [NAS.RH1.2.908][IJ:7.5.1841]

LADY HANNAH ELLICE, 345 tons, master J. Liddell, from Greenock *with passengers* bound for New York on 10 September 1834. [AJ#4518][GkAd#5008]

LADY HARVEY, Captain Douglas, from the Clyde to California on 7 September 1849. [EEC#21861]

LADY HOOD, bound for Cape Breton *with 78 passengers* before 1828. [TGSI#55.341]

LADY KINNAIRD, from Dundee to New York in July 1839. [EEC#19935]; 350 tons, master John S. Robb, from Dundee to Montreal *with 65 passengers* on 18 April 1843, [BPP.35.503][DW#118]

LADY KNIGHT, from the Clyde to Boston in August 1850. [EEC#22014]

LADY MARY FOX, 350 tons, Captain Lightbody, from Glasgow *with passengers* bound for Prince Edward Island on 8 April 1844. [GSP#848]

LADY OF THE LAKE, Captain Stephen, from Leith to Quebec on 2 September 1830. [LCL#1828]

LADY OF THE LAKE, 424 tons, from Greenock *with 6 passengers* bound for New Brunswick in Spring 1832, [CM#17337]; Captain Hugh Munn, from Greenock *with passengers* bound for New York on 20 June 1838, [AJ#4717][SG#7/672]; Captain Thomas Jamieson, from Glasgow *with 94 passengers* bound for New York by 4 April 1842; from Glasgow *with passengers* bound for New York on 25 July 1842. [GSP#705/712/824]; Captain Smith from Glasgow to New York 7 June 1849.[EEC#21837] [SG#18/1824]

LADY OF THE LAKE, Captain Taylor, from Glasgow to St Andrews, New Brunswick, in July 1849; from the Clyde to Newfoundland on 17 August 1850; Captain Duncan, from the Clyde to Boston on 24 February 1853. [EEC#21822/21835/22007/22401]

LADY OF THE LAKE, 424 tons, master Thomas Jameson, from Glasgow **with passengers** to New York in February 1842, [GH#4068]; Captain Duncan, from the Clyde to Quebec on 17 August 1850; from the Clyde to Boston on 4 March 1851. [EEC#22007/22091]

LADY OF THE WEST, from the Clyde to Quebec in August 1850. [EEC#22013]

LADY OF THE LAKE, Collings, from Leith to Quebec 9 April 1857. [LCL#4603]

LADY SALE, Captain Perry, from the Clyde to Boston on 5 August 1849, [EEC#21846]

LADY SEATON, 370 tons, from Glasgow **with passengers** bound for Charleston on 15 September 1841. [GSP#682]

LADY TURNER, Captain George, from Greenock **with 6 pasengers** bound for Newfoundland on 20 April 1839. [SG#8/763]

LANARKSHIRE OF GLASGOW, to Quebec in June 1849, [EEC#21838]

LANCASHIRE, 661 tons, Captain Alexander, from Glasgow to New York on 1 June 1841; Captain Lyon, from Glasgow **with passengers** bound for New York on 3 August 1842. [GSP#666/826]

LARNE, 577 tons, Captain Robertson, from Leith to Quebec on 30 June 1854; from Leith to St John, New Brunswick, on 30 June 1855; Captain Lindegreen, from Leith to Quebec 30 March 1857; from Leith to Quebec April 1860.[LCL#4314/4600/4916] [EEC#22758]

LAUREL, 808 tons brig, Captain Walker, from Glasgow **with passengers** bound for Quebec on 25 June 1844. [GSP#861]; arrived in Quebec on 12 May 1846 **with 3 passengers** from Glasgow. [MT]

LAUSANNE, a 400 ton American ship, Captain Mercy, from Glasgow **with passengers** bound for New York on 28 March 1843. [GSP#779]

LEANDER, Captain Wilkie, from Greenock to Newfoundland 14 September 1834. [GkAd#5011]

LEDA, Captain Lyell, arrived in New York on 9 October 1834 from Dundee. [AJ#4531]

LEILA, 614 tons, Captain Higgins, from Glasgow to Baltimore on 8 June 1841. [GSP#666]

LEIPSIC, a 450 ton barque, Captain John Ritchie, from Dundee **with passengers** bound for New York on 30 June 1842. [FJ#494];

from Dundee to Canada **with 5 passengers** on 3 April 1843.
[BPP.35.503][DW#106]

LEO, 250 tons, Captain Murphy, from Glasgow **with passengers** bound for Quebec and Montreal in April 1843. [GSP#796]

LEODES, a 490 ton American ship, Captain Robins, from Glasgow **with passengers** bound for Boston on 16 May 1844. [GSP#851]

LEOPARD, from the Clyde bound for New Orleans in March 1843.[EEC#20594]

LESMAHAGOW, Captain Giben, from the Clyde to St John, New Brunswick, on 29 May 1851, [EEC#22127]

LESOSTRIS, arrived in Boston **with passengers** on 17 May 1850 from Glasgow. [USNA/par]

LETITIA, Captain Barker, from the Clyde to Boston on 8 April 1851, [EEC#22106]

LEVANT, 400 tons, Captain Whitesley, from Glasgow **with passengers** bound for New York on 26 April 1843. [GSP#800]; Captain Reid, from the Clyde to Pictou on 4 July 1847; Captain Aury, from the Clyde to New York on 5 June 1851. [EEC#21523/22130]

LEVEN LASS, from the Clyde to Quebec in June 1840. [EEC#20272]

LIBERTY, 662 tons, Captain Morton, from Glasgow **with passengers** bound for New York on 10 June 1844. [GSP#860]; from the Clyde to New York in June 1850; Captain Peabody, from the Clyde to New York on 11 October 1850; from the Clyde to New York on 22 February 1851, arrived in New York on 4 April 1851. [EEC#21985/22032/22087/22110]

LION, Captain McKenzie, from Aberdeen to St John, New Brunswick, on 10 April 1848; from Aberdeen to Quebec on 19 April 1850; Captain Morrison, from Aberdeen to Quebec on 16 April 1851, arrived there on 26 May 1851; from Aberdeen to Quebec 15 April 1853; Captain Clegg, from Aberdeen to Quebec 26 April 1858, [CM#21403][EEC#21644/21959/22110][AJ#5397] [LCL#3877/3979/4188]

LISKEARD, a barque, from Loch Hourn **with 344 passengers from Glenelg** bound for Quebec on 13 July 1849; **with 104 passengers from Barra and South Uist** bound for Canada in 1851. [GHF#323/326] [TGSI#55.340] [SRO.HD21/22][W,21.7.1849] [S,21.7.1849]

LIVERPOOL, 600 tons, Captain Swanford, from Glasgow to New Orleans on 22 September 1840; from Glasgow **with passengers** bound for Quebec on 25 April 1843. [GSP#693/779/800]; Captain Mackay, from Grangemouth to St John's, New Brunswick, on 22 July 1850; from Grangemouth to Quebec on 3 April 1851. [EEC#21997/22105][LCL#3974];

Captain Mackay, from Grangemouth to Quebec on 13 April
1858, [CM#21391]

LOCHLIBO, 1006 tons, Captain Taylor, from Glasgow *with
passengers* bound for New York on 6 May 1842. [GSP#715]

LOIS, Captain Croker, from the Clyde to Boston on 27 June 1850.
[EEC#21985]

LONDON, a 240 ton barque, Captain Brown, from Greenock to
Pictou, Nova Scotia, on 10 July 1845, SG#14/1419]; from
Greenock *with 50 passengers* to Pictou in May 1847,
[EEC#21517]; Captain John McDonald, from Glasgow on 11
April 1848 *with 36 passengers* bound for Pictou, Nova
Scotia, and on 14 July 1848 *with 26
passengers.*[SG#17/1699, 1732]
[PANS#RG1.257.104/131][EEC#21644][PB#114]

LONDONDERRY, from the Clyde to Quebec in June 1853.
[EEC#22454]

LORD BROUGHAM, a brig, from Inverness *with passengers*
bound for Nova Scotia, arrived in Pictou in September 1831.
[CP:10 September 1831]

LORD BYRON, Captain McBride, from Greenock to Miramachi on 26
July 1838, [SG#7/685]; Captain Todd, from the Clyde to
Quebec on 28 July 1845, [SG#14/1422]; Captain Campbell,
from the Clyde to Quebec on 1 August 1849; from the Clyde to
Quebec in August 1855; Captain Moodie, from the Clyde to
Quebec March 1858. [EEC#21844/322776][CM#21381]

LORD METCALFE, a 510 ton barque, Captain William Rosie, from
Aberdeen *with passengers* bound for Quebec on 15 April
1847, arrived there on 27 May 1850; from Aberdeen to Quebec
on 18 August 1847, [AJ#5175/5189/5194]; from Aberdeen to
Quebec on 10 April 1848. [EEC#21644]; Captain Young, from
Troon to Quebec 16 April 1858, [CM#21394]

LORD MULGRAVE OF WHITBY, 414 tons, arrived in Prince Edward
Island during 1830 from Scotland. [TIM#17.34]

LORD PANMURE, 450 tons, master John McNeill, from Dundee *with
passengers* bound for Quebec and Montreal in July 1840;
arrived in Quebec on 11 September from Dundee.
[S#24/2140][AJ#4842]

LORD SEATON OF QUEBEC, a bark, Captain William Talbot, from
Scrabster to Quebec on 11 April 1841, [LCL#3458]; from
Aberdeen via Cromarty, and Scrabster, Caithness, 16 April 1845
with 72 passengers from Caithness and Orkney bound
for Canada, arrived in Quebec on 16 May 1845; from Aberdeen
on 3 August 1845 *with 64 passengers* bound for Quebec,
arrived there September 1845; from Scrabster/Thurso *with 20
passengers* bound for Canada on 11 April 1846, arrived in

Quebec on 18 May 1846, [QG][MT]; from Aberdeen to Quebec on 16 March 1847; from Montrose to Quebec on 12 April 1849; from Aberdeen to Quebec on 11 April 1850, arrived there on 15 May 1850; from Aberdeen via Peterhead to Quebec on 16 August 1850; Captain Mann, from Dundee to Quebec on 3 April 1851. [FAO#71][AJ#5135/5176][EEC#21798] [EEC#21955/21976/22004/22007/22104] [AJ,14.5.1845][FAO#1/70/88][Que.Gaz.10.9.1845]

LORD SIDMOUTH, 595 ton barque, Captain Sangster, from Greenock to Quebec in April 1839, [SG#8/762]; Captain S. Bryan, from Port Glasgow *with passengers* bound for St John, New Brunswick, on 20 May 1842, *"a most desirable opportunity for passengers for the above port as well as the adjacent ports and places in New Brunswick, Nova Scotia, the United States and Canada, there being frequent and easy connections to these places from St John"*, [GSP#716], arrived there on 1 July 1842; from Glasgow to Prince Edward Island, arrived there 13 October 1846; Captain Dow, from the Clyde to Pictou on 5 July 1847.[EEC#21523]; Captain Fraser, from the Clyde to Quebec 6 April 1858. [CM#21385]

LOTUS, Captain Pollock, from the Clyde to Montreal on 12 May 1850; Captain Watson, from the Clyde to New Orleans on 16 November 1850; Captain Brown, arrived in Boston 20 December 1860 from the Clyde. [EEC#21967/22044][S#1737]

LOUISA, Captain Hume, from Greenock to St John's, New Brunswick, wrecked off Barrington in April 1832. [CM#17304]

LOUISA, Captain McAlpin, from the Clyde to Nova Scotia on 11 April 1848. [EEC#21644]

LOYAL TAR, from Stromness to Quebec in May 1840. [EEC#20070]

LUCIUS CARY, from Glasgow, arrived in Pictou on 3 June 1847. [EEC#21521]

LUCONIA, 480 tons, Captain Porter, from Glasgow *with passengers* bound for Baltimore on 12 June 1844. [GSP#860]

LUCY, 400 tons, from Glasgow to New York on 28 September 1840. [GSP#693]

LULAN OF PICTOU, a 472 ton barque, Captain George MacKenzie, from Glasgow and the Outer Hebrides *with 120 passengers from Barra and South Uist* bound for Canada, arrived in Pictou, Nova Scotia, on 11 August 1848, *72 passengers* moved to Charlottetown, Prince Edward Island, on 18 November 1848. Captain Chisholm, from the Clyde to Pictou on 24 May 1849; from the Clyde to New York on 14 May 1850; from the Clyde to Savannah on 7 December 1850; from the Clyde to Boston on 21 May 1851. [GHF#325][PAPEI]

[CNSHS#23.46]
[PANS.RG1.257.167][EEC.21814/21967/22054/22124]
LUNA, a brig, master T. Lookup, from Dumfries to Richibucto, New
Brunswick, in 1830, [DCr: 10.8.1830]; from Glencaple to New
Brunswick in 1831, [DCr: 3.1.1831]; arrived in Prince Edward
Island by 24 May 1831 from Dumfries. [TIM#17.34]
LUNAN, a 500 ton barque, master W.Brown, from Leith *with
passengers* bound for Quebec and Montreal on 6 April 1854.
[EEC#22537][LCL#4290]
LYDIA, Captain Trask, from the Clyde to New York on 4 April 1850;
from the Clyde to Boston on 21 March 1850; from the Clyde to
Boston on 24 August 1850; from the Clyde to Boston on 1
March 1851 [EEC#21950/22009/22090/22099]
LYDIA, Captain Soule, from the Clyde to New York on 24 August
1850. [EEC#22009]
LYRA, Captain Park, from the Clyde to Montreal on 25 August 1849.
[EEC#21855]
MABEL, from the Clyde to Richebucto in September 1854.
[EEC#22640]
MADEIRA, Captain Ross, from the Clyde to Newfoundland, arrived
there on 21 May 1833. [SG#2/151]
MADONNA, Captain Smith, from Glasgow *with 3 passengers*
bound for Newfoundland on 13 April 1839; from Glasgow to
Newfoundland on 1 October 1839. [SG#8/760; 8/808]
MADURA, Captain Pinkerton, from the Clyde to San Francisco on 26
February 1851. [EEC#21088]
MAGNET, Captain Wallace, from Leith *with passengers* bound for
Quebec 8 June 1831. [EEC#18684][LCL#1908]
MAGOG, Captain Kennedy, from Glasgow to Quebec on 13 April
1839, [SG#8/760]; Captain Shanks, from Ayr to St John's, New
Brunswick, on 12 July 1849; Captain Russell, from Ayr to St
John's, New Brunswick, arrived there on 18 May 1850; from
Ayr to Quebec in September 1854. [EEC#21838/21976/22639]
MAHAICA OF GREENOCK, a barque, Captain Jump, from Greenock
to Quebec and Montreal on 17 May 1839, [SG#8/771]; from
Glasgow bound for Montreal in June 1843. [EEC#20624]
MAID OF THE MILL, from the Clyde to California in June 1853.
[EEC#22475]
MAJESTIC, Captain Lawson, from Dundee to New York on 27
January 1830; from Dundee to New York on 12 August 1830.
[PA#26/54]; Captain Forbes, arrived in Quebec on 10 October
1834 from Dundee. [AJ#4532]
MAJESTIC, 500 tons, from Glasgow to St John's, New Brunswick, in
April 1841, [GSP#657]

MAJESTIC OF SHIELDS, from Glasgow to Quebec in August 1854.
[EC#22627]

MALABAR, Captain Fraser, from the Clyde to New York on 29 April
1849; from the Clyde to Quebec on 7 April 1850; Captain
Crocker, from the Clyde to New Orleans on 31 March 1851.
[EEC#21804/21951/22102]

MALLAIGA, a 281 ton barque, master William Gump, arrived in New
York on 5 March 1842 *with 4 passengers* from Glasgow.
[USNA.M237/48]

MALORY, a brig, arrived in Sydney, Cape Breton Island, on 28
August 1830 *with 211 passengers* from Scotland.
[PANS.Ass.Mss.Misc.B]

MANCHESTER, 570 tons, Captain R. Bosworth, from Glasgow to
Boston on 25 April 1841. [GSP#661]

MANDANE, Captain Hutchison, from the Clyde to Quebec on 14
August 1850. [EEC#22005]

MARCHIONESS OF ABERCORN, 875 tons, from Glasgow to
Quebec in April 1841, [GSP#657]

MARCHIONESS OF CLYDESDALE, Captain Ferguson, from the
Clyde to New York on 16 May 1850; from the Clyde on 26 April
1851 to New York, [EEC#21968/22114]; from Greenock *with
32 passengers* bound for New York, arrived there on 6
December 1852. [USNA]

MARCHIONESS OF QUEENSBERRY, Captain McCallum, from Leith
to Quebec on 31 March 1841, [LCL#3452]; from the Clyde to
Quebec on 15 September 1849. [EEC#21864]

MARCHMONT, Captain White, from the Clyde to Quebec on 31
August 1850. [EEC#22013]

MARENGO, Captain Gillespie, from Glasgow to New York on 30 May
1839, [SG#8/774]

MARGARET, a 200 ton brig, Captain D. Smith, from Leith to
Miramachi on 8 April 1829, [LCL#1682]; from Leven *with
passengers* bound for Montreal on 2 April 1833.
[Times#15146][FJ#14][FH#574]

MARGARET, Captain Miller, from Greenock to St John, New
Brunswick, on 21 August 1839, [SG#8/798]; Captain Henry
Betts, from Greenock *with 8 passengers* bound for St John,
New Brunswick, arrived there on 9 November 1833. [PANB]

MARGARET, a brig, Captain Naith, from Leith *with passengers*
bound for Quebec and Montreal on 1 April 1839. [EEC#19871]

MARGARET, a barque, from Greenock *with passengers* bound for
Quebec in July 1843. [LCL#171]

MARGARET, 623 tons, from Glasgow to Canada *with 238
passengers* on 30 June 1843, [BPP.35.503]

MARGARET, Captain Harrison, from the Clyde to New York on 15
  April 1848; Captain Webster, from the Clyde to New York on 24
  September 1849. EEC#21645/21868]
MARGARET, Captain Norris, from the Clyde to New York on 15
  August 1849. [EEC#21850]
MARGARET BALFOUR, from Dundee *with 80 passengers from
  Logie Almond, Perthshire,* bound for Quebec in April 1830.
  [DA, 8.4.1830]; Captain Robert Laurie, from Glasgow *with
  passengers* bound for Quebec and Montreal during July 1833,
  from Greenock to Quebec on 16 April 1834, [SG#2/147;
  3/237]; Captain Fitzsimmons, from Greenock to Quebec on 26
  July 1838, [SG#7/685]
MARGARET BOGLE OF LEITH, a 320 ton barque, master Walter
  Smith, from Leith *with 22 passengers* to Quebec on 6 April
  1829, [LCL#1682]; from Leith to Miramachi on 14 August
  1830, [LCL#1823]; from Leith to Miramachi in March 1831,
  [LCL#1887]; from Leith to Miramachi in July 1832,
  [LCL#2027]; from Leith *with 70 passengers* for Quebec in
  April 1833. [Times#15137][LCL#2099]; from Leith *with 49
  passengers* to Quebec 9 April 1834, [LCL#2204]; from Leith
  with 54 passengers to New York 1 April 1835, [LCL#2306];
  from Leith *with 120 passengers* bound for Quebec in May
  1837, [LCL#2680]; from Invergordon *with passengers* bound
  for Quebec on 1 June 1837, arrived in Quebec on 30 June 1837
  from Leith, [AJ#4658/4674]; from Leith *with passengers*
  bound for Montreal and Quebec on 27 May 1841, [FH#998];
  Captain D.Morrison, from Leith *with passengers* bound for
  Montreal on 10 May 1843. [EEC#20192/20590][LCL#3152]
MARGARET DEWER, Captain Joye, from the Clyde to New York on
  16 July 1851, [EEC#22148]
MARGARET PAYNTER, a 137 ton barque, master James Reece,
  arrived in New York on 9 April 1842 *with 5 passengers* from
  Glasgow. [USNA.M237/48]
MARGARET POLLOCK, 800 tons, from Glasgow to Prince Edward
  Island in April 1841, [GSP#657]
MARGARET POYNTER, 305 tons, master John McIsaac, from
  Glasgow *with passengers* to New York in January 1842,
  [GH#4062]; from Glasgow to Canada *with 51 passengers*
  on 10 August 1843, [BPP.35.503]
MARGARET RITCHIE OF SALTCOATS, Captain Robert Clark, from
  Ardrossan to Chaleur Bay, lost at sea on 10 May 1833.
  [SG#2/156]
MARGARET SCOTT, from the Clyde to Quebec in August 1843.
  [EEC#20648]

MARGARET THOMSON, a 212 ton brig, Captain Galloway, from Leith **with passengers** bound for Montreal on 30 July 1851, [EEC#22148]

MARIA BRENNAN, 250 tons, Captain Milligan, from Glasgow **with passengers** bound for Quebec and Montreal in April 1843. [GSP#796]

MARINER, Captain Wallace, from Dundee to Miramachi on 5 April 1830. [PA#35]; Captain Taylor, from Greenock to Quebec on 3 April 1839, [SG#8.757]

MARINER, Captain Campbell, from the Clyde to Miramachi on 14 July 1849; from the Clyde to Miramachi on 3 April 1850; from the Clyde to Bathurst on 11 July 1850; from the Clyde to Miramachi on 3 July 1851. [EEC#21837/21950/21992/22142]

MARION, Captain Parsons, from Greenock to New York on 4 July 1839, [SG#8/785]

MARJORY, a 300 ton brig, Captain James Stocks, from Leith **with 24 passengers** bound for Quebec and Montreal on 21 June 1833. [FH#587][FJ#23][LCL#2121]

MARQUIS OF STAFFORD, from Isle of Lewis **with 500 passengers** bound for Canada via Troon in May 1851. [GHF#219/325]

MARS, Captain Mitchell, from Leith to Miramachi on 3 April 1829. [LCL#1681]

MARS, Captain Castle, from Greenock to New Orleans on 3 March 1839, [SG#8/748]

MARS, 405 tons, Captain Robert Robertson, from Greenock **with passengers** bound for Boston on 25 May 1844. [GSP#854]; from Greenock to New Orleans **with passengers** in April 1844. [DW#167]

MARS, Captain Younger, from Montrose to Quebec 6 April 1840, [LCL]; Captain Carstairs, from Montrose to Quebec on 3 April 1851; from Grangemouth to Quebec 2 April 1854. [EEC#22104][LCL#3976/4289]

MARTHA'S VINYARD, Captain Pye, from the Clyde to New York on 14 May 1850; Captain Higgins, from the Clyde to New York on 20 September 1850; Captain Griffiths, from the Clyde to New York on 22 May 1851. [EEC#21967/22021/22126]

MARY, arrived in Prince Edward Island by 24 August 1830 **with passengers** from Tobermory, Mull. [TIM#17.33]

MARY, Captain Ritchie, from the Clyde to the Bay of Chaleur in August 1832. [CM#17342]

MARY, Captain Rosey, from Aberdeen to Cape Breton Island in 1834. [AJ#4515]

MARY, 364 tons, from Glasgow **with passengers** bound for New York on 15 May 1841. [GSP#662]; CaptainWade, arrived in

Montreal on 7 October 1844 **with 9 passengers**, [MT]; Captain R. D. Munro, from Glasgow **with passengers** bound for Montreal on 15 July 1848; Captain Moore, from the Clyde to Montreal on 16 August 1849; Captain Watson, from the Clyde to Montreal on 12 April 1851.[SG#17/1694] [EEC#21672/21850/22108]

MARY, Captain Moses, from the Clyde to New York on 16 June 1849. [EEC#21825]

MARY ANNE, arrived in Prince Edward Island on 12 September 1831 **with passengers,** some landed at Point Prim before the ship sailed west. [TIM#1.34]; from Stornaway **with 121 passengers** bound for Nova Scotia, landed at Sydney, Cape Breton Island, on 10 July 1832. [PANS#282/48]

MARY ANN, Captain Childs, from the Clyde **with passengers** bound for New York in 1838, took refuge in Londonderry as storm-damaged. [AJ#4735]

MARY ANN, Captain Bisset, from the Clyde to St John, New Brunswick, on 21 July 1845, [SG#14/1422]; Captain Waddington, from the Clyde to Boston on 25 September 1849. [EEC#21868]

MARY ANNE CLINTON, 500 tons, from Glasgow to Quebec in July 1840. [GSP#681]

MARY ANN HATTON, 567 tons, from Glasgow to Quebec in July 1840. [GSP#681]

MARY ANNE HENRY, 491 tons, Captain Nichol or Rey, from Glasgow **with passengers** bound for Halifax on 25 July 1844. [GSP#866]

MARY CAMPBELL, 300 tons, from Glasgow to St John's, New Brunswick, in April 1841, [GSP#657]; Captain Guthrie, from the Clyde to St John's, New Brunswick, on 23 September 1849; Captain Bullan, from the Clyde to St Andrew's, New Brunswick, on 2 September 1850. [EEC#21867/22013]

MARY DOROTHY, from Bo'ness to Quebec in April 1851. [EEC#22120]

MARY EMMA, Captain Lucas, from the Clyde to Boston on 18 September 1850. [EEC#22020]

MARY KENNEDY, arrived in Prince Edward Island during 1830 **with 80 passengers** from Tobermory, Mull; arrived in Prince Edward Island during 1831 **with 80 passengers** from the Hebrides. [TIM#17.34/35]

MARY KINGSLAND, 839 tons, from Glasgow to New York on 13 March 1841. [GSP#655]

MARY MAC, Captain Melanon, from Ardrosan to Boston in March 1853. [EEC#22456]

MARY MORRIS OF NEW YORK, a 394 ton barque, Captain Philander Doggett, from the Clyde to New York on 21 April 1848; from the Clyde *with passengers* to New York on 8 June 1849; from the Clyde to New York on 16 March 1850; from the Clyde to New York on 13 July 1850; Captain Peter Proteau, from the Clyde to New York on 8 April 1851. [EEC#21649/21822/21942/ 21993/ 22106]; master Peter Proteau, arrived in New York on 28 June 1852 *with 212 passengers* from Glasgow. [USNA.M237/115]; Captain Freeman, from the Clyde to New York in May 1853; Captain McLeary, from the Clyde *with passengers* bound for New York, at Stranraer on 10 February 1854, arrived in New York in August 1854 [EEC#22444/22542/22640][SG#18/1860]

MARY PRING, a 263 ton brig, Captain Todd, from Glasgow *with passengers* bound for St Johns, New Brunswick, on 30 May 1839. [SG#8/762, 773]

MASONIC, Captain Heckman, from the Clyde to Boston on 16 August 1849; arrived in Boston on 22 April 1850 from Troon. [EEC#21850/21966]

MATTHEW, a brig, from Kirkcudbright to Richibucto in 1830. [DCr:11.5.1830]

MAXIM, a 300 ton barque, Captain Crombie, from Leith to Montreal on 12 April 1853. [EEC#22396][LCL#4187]

MAYFLOWER, 507 tons, Captain McKnight, from Glasgow to New York on 22 April 1841. [GSP#661]; from Troon to New York in April 1849; from the Clyde to New Orleans on 10 February 1853. [EEC#21796/22393]

MEANWELL, 400 tons, from Glasgow to Quebec in April 1841. [GSP#657]

MEARNS, Captain Smith, from the Clyde to Mobile on 26 October 1850; from Glasgow to Quebec in June 1854. [EEC#22036/22600]

MEDFORD, a 600 ton American ship, Captain Wilbur, from Glasgow *with passengers* bound for New Orleans on 20 September 1842. [GSP#771]

MEDIUM, Captain Crosby, from the Clyde to Boston on 16 August 1850. [EEC#22007]

MEDORA, a 600 ton American ship, Captain George Lunt, from Dundee *with passengers* bound for New York on 15 July 1842. [FJ#49]

MEG MERRILEES, from Campbelltown to New York in July 1849. [EEC#21837]

MELISSA, from Lewis *with 330 passengers* bound for Canada in 1855. [GHF#325]

MELPOMEME, Captain Beveridge, from the Clyde to Quebec in July 1832. [CM#17326]; from the Clyde to Quebec, lost at sea on 27 April 1833. [SG#2/151]

MEMPHIS, a 800 ton American ship, from Glasgow to New York on 7 July 1840; Captain Knight, from Glasgow *with passengers* bound for New York on 28 March 1843. [GSP#681/779]

MENAPIA, 280 tons, from Glasgow to Canada *with 183 passengers* on 13 June 1843, [BPP.35.503]

MERCATOR, a 287 ton brig, Captain James Marshall, arrived in Pictou during 1832 *with 131 passengers* from Greenock; from Greenock *with 5 passengers* bound for Pictou on 25 March 1834, [SG#2/222]; from Greenock *with 6 passengers* bound for Pictou on 17 July 1834, [SG#3/270]; arrived in Pictou on 18 August 1834 *with 5 passengers* from Greenock. [PANS#282/118]

MERLIN, Captain Corbin, from the Clyde to St John, Newfoundland, on 9 May 1850. [EEC#21964/21978]

MERSEY, 350 tons, Captain Williams, from Glasgow *with passengers* bound for New York on 1 September 1840. [GSP#690]

MERSEY, 786 tons, Captain Rae, from Greenock *with passengers* bound for New York on 14 June 1842; Captain Hugh Reid, from Greenock *with passengers* bound for New York on 16 August 1842. [GSP#718/826]

METEOR FLAG, Captain Fraser, from the Clyde to Pictou in April 1858. [CM#21388]

MICHIGAN, 498 tons, Captain Sturges, from Glasgow *with passengers* bound for New Orleans on 16 August 1841; Captain Hasty, from Glasgow *with passengers* bound for Boston/New York on 24 January 1842. *"times of sailing have been chosen to enable emigrants to reach their destination at the beginning of the season when wages are at their highest and rates of passage half the usual later in the season"*.[GSP#676/700][GH#4062]; Captain Mason, from Greenock to Boston on 7 August 1845, [SG#14/1427]

MICMAC, Captain Auld, from the Clyde to Boston on 28 August 1849; from the Clyde to Halifax on 20 March 1850; from the Clyde to New York in May 1850; from the Clyde to Charleston on 25 March 1850; from the Clyde to Halifax on 29 August 1850; from Scotland *with passengers* to Halifax, Nova Scotia, in September 1851; Captain McNutt, from the Clyde to Montreal in April 1858. [Coll.NSHS#39/162] [EEC#21855/21943/21980/22100/22012][CM#21399]

MIDDLESBRO, a 245 ton brig, Captain R. Monro, from Leith to
Quebec and Montreal on 5 April 1847; from Leith to Quebec
and Montreal in April 1848. [EEC#21468/21613]

MIDDLESEX, a 540 ton American ship, Captain Grozier, from
Glasgow *with passengers* bound to Boston on 25 September
1842. [GSP#771]

MIDLOTHIAN, Captain Morrison, from Loch Snizort, Skye, *with
passengers from Lorgill, Glendale,* bound for Nova Scotia
1844.[PGSI.55.331]

MILFORD, a 324 ton barque, Captain William Rees, from Leith and
Dundee *with passengers* bound for New York on 5 June
1840. [EEC#20206]

MILO, Captain Corning, from the Clyde to Miramachi April 1858.
[CM#21388]

MILTON, a brig, Captain Anderson, from Aberdeen to Sydney, Cape
Breton, on 9 May 1841, [LCL#3464]; from Aberdeen *with
passengers* bound for Sydney, Cape Breton, on 1 May 1846.
[AJ#5128]

MINERVA, Captain Adamson, from Leith *with 58 passengers* to
Quebec 7 June 1833, arrived there on 8 August 1833.
[LCL#2117][FH#603]

MINERVA, Captain Miller, from Ayr to St John, New Brunswick, on 12
July 1849, [EEC#21838]; Captain Shank, from Troon to
Philadelphia on 11 March 1850; from Troon to San Francisco on
24 August 1850; [S#3151/3531] [EEC#21940/22010]; Captain
Stewart, from the Clyde to Montreal on 19 April 1851.
[EEC#222111]; from Troon to New York in August 1854,
[EEC#22633]; Captain McFarlane, from Ayr to St Johns, New
Brunswick, 16 June 1858, [CM#21445]; Captain MacFarlane,
arrived in Savannah 5 January 1861 from Ayr. [S#1749]

MINSTREL, 450 tons, from Glasgow to Quebec on 10 April 1841,
[GSP#659]

MIRAMACHI, from the Clyde bound for North America in May 1843;
Captain Main, from the Clyde to St John's, New Brunswick, on
12 June 1849; from the Clyde to Quebec on 1 April 1850.
[EEC#20610/21823/21948]

MISSISSIPPI, 850 tons, Captain Hieland, from Glasgow *with
passengers* bound for New York on 19 April 1843.
[GSP#800]; Captain Henrici, from Glasgow to New York on 22
April 1850, arrived *with passengers* 21 May 1850; Captain
Hardie, from the Clyde to New York on 16 November 1850.
[EEC#21957/22045]

MOHAWK, from Glasgow *with 51 passengers* bound for Canada
by 4 April 1842. [GSP#712]

MOLSON, a 350 ton brig, Captain Law, from Dundee to Quebec on 2 June 1830. [PA#44]; Captain James Elliot, from Dundee via Aberdeen *with 89 passengers* bound for Quebec and Montreal on 26 July 1834. [AJ#4514/4516]

MONARCH OF IRVINE, 315 tons, Captain Douglas, from Glasgow *with 13 passengers* bound for Quebec and Montreal on 13 July 1839, [SG#8/787]; from Glasgow to Montreal and Quebec in March 1845. [EEC#21159]; Captain Allan, from Greenock to Montreal on 31 July 1845, [SG#14/1425]

MONARCH, Captain Marshall, from Dundee to Quebec 7 April 1840. [LCL]

MONONAGHELA, 507 tons, from Glasgow to Philadelphia on 8 March 1841. [GSP#655]

MONTEZUMA, 500 tons, from Glasgow to Philadelphia on 22 September 1840, [GSP#693]; from Glasgow *with passengers* bound for Quebec ? on 7 May 1843, on 7 September 1843, and on 7 January 1844, [GSP#799]; *with 442 passengers from Barra and South Uist* bound for Canada in 1851. [GHF#326]

MONTROSE, 736 tons, Captain Huie, from Leith to St John, New Brunswick, on 26 March 1853. [LCL#4182]

MONUMENT, 500 tons, Captain Chase, from Glasgow to New Orleans in 1841. [GSP#653]; from Glasgow to Canada *with 87 passengers* on 28 June 1843, [BPP.35.503]

MORGIANA, 300 tons, Captain Sullivan, from Glasgow *with passengers* bound for Prince Edward Island on 10 April 1844. [GSP#848]

MORO, Captain Larrabec, from the Clyde to New York on 31 August 1850. [EEC#22013]

MOSCOW, from Greenock *with 83 passengers* bound for New York in April 1833. [Times#15146]

MOSLEM, 450 tons, from Glasgow to New York on 10 July 1840. [GSP#681]

MOUNTAINEER, 869 tons, Captain Stickney, from Glasgow to Quebec on 15 June 1842, [GSP#719]; Captain Smith, from the Clyde to Quebec on 10 April 1850. [EEC#21952]

MOUNT STEWART ELPHINSTONE OF GLASGOW, 387 tons, from the Clyde *with passengers* bound for New York on 1 February 1849, storm damaged returned to Greenock; from the Clyde to New York on 17 March 1849; Captain Stewart from the Clyde via Lochboisdale on 14 July 1849 *with 250 passengers from Barra and South Uist* bound to Montreal and Quebec in August 1849; Captain Henderson, from the Clyde to New York on 12 May 1850. [GHF#325] [SG#18/1830] [EEC#21773/21786/21837/21847/21967]

MOZAMBIQUE, Captain Gillies, from Greenock *with 1 passenger* bound for St Johns, New Brunswick, on 30 June 1838; from Greenock to St John, New Brunswick, on 4 March 1839; from Glasgow to St John, New Brunswick, on 30 May 1839. [SG#7/679; 8/748; 8/773]

MUNRO, a 225 ton brig, Captain John Finlay, from Leith *with 10 passengers* bound for Montreal on 5 April 1840; Captain Frederick Scott, from Leith *with 10 passengers* bound for Montreal on 5 April 1850, arrived there 20 May 1850. [LCL#3874/3879] [S#3145][EEC#21938/21946/21954/21978] [

NAIAD, Captain Brown, arrived in Quebec on 10 October 1834 from Ross. [AJ#4532]; from Troon to Quebec in July 1854. [EEC#22618]

NAILER, 312 tons, master Alexander McCall, from Greenock *with passengers* to Quebec in April 1831, [GkAd#3628]; from Greenock *with 23 passengers* bound for Canada in April 1833. [Times#15146]

NANCY, Captain Graham, from Grangemouth to Quebec 31 March 1840. [LCL#2828]

NAPOLEON, 540 tons, Captain Sherman, from Glasgow to New York on 5 May 1840. [GSP#673]

NATIVITY, from Glasgow to Montreal on 20 April 1841, [GSP#659]

NAVARINO, an American ship, Captain Stephen Carmick, from Glasgow *with passengers* bound for New York in April 1843. [GSP#793]

NELSON, a brig, from Maryport *with 158 passengers from Dumfries and Galloway* bound for Quebec in June 1834. [Dumfries Courier, 11.6.1834]

NELSON WOOD, 309 tons, Captain Ball, from Glasgow *with passengers* bound for Quebec on 10 July 1842. [GSP#724]

NEPTUNE, 400 tons, Captain James Brown, from Leith *with 116 passengers* bound for Montreal on 9 April 1830, [LCL#1787]; from Leith *with 113 passengers* bound for Montreal and Quebec on 28 March 1831, arrived on 24 May 1831. [EEC#18603/18671][LCL#1889]

NEPTUNE, Captain Cumming, from Aberdeen to Miramachi on 17 May 1840. [AJ#4819]

NEPTUNE, 360 tons, Captain Reichenberg, from Glasgow *with passengers* bound for New York on 26 March 1844. [GSP#841]

NERO, a brig, from Greenock *with passengers* bound for Pictou, Nova Scotia, in 1829.

NEVA, 500 tons, Captain Bunker, from Glasgow to New York on 29 March 1841, [GSP#657]

NEW BRUNSWICK, 414 tons, Captain Edward Hunter, from Glasgow *with passengers* bound for New York on 25 May 1842; from Glasgow *with passengers* bound for New York on 22 June 1842. *"this superb ship carries a surgeon and a clergyman"*. [GSP#716/721]

NEW ENGLAND, 357 tons, from Glasgow *with passengers* bound for Boston on 18 September 1840, [GSP#691]; from Glasgow *with passengers* bound for America in April 1853. [Fife Advertiser#398]

NEWTON, from the Clyde to Quebec in July 1839. [EEC#19935]

NEW YORK, 1000 tons, Captain Barston, from Glasgow to New York on 7 June 1840; from Glasgow to New York on 7 October 1840; Captain Cropper, from Glasgow *with passengers* bound for New York on 17 October 1841; Captain John Niven, from Glasgow *with passengers* bound for New York in August 1842; Captain Cropper, from Glasgow *with passengers* bound for New York on 7 October 1842; from Glasgow *with passengers* to New York on 7 February 1843 and on 7 June 1843.
[GSP#678/684/693/773/791/826][DW#121]

NEW YORK PACKET, 1000 tons, Captain J. Farquharson, from the Clyde to Boston on 2 June 1849; from Greenock *with passengers* bound for New Orleans on 30 October 1849, *"the best and cheapest route to the Western States"*, [SG#18/1863]; master William Muir, from Glasgow *with passengers* bound for New York on 31 March 1851, arrived there in May 1851; from Glasgow *with passengers* bound for New York in September 1854.
[EEC#21819/22102/22619][USNA.M333.4.10]

NEW YORK, a 2050 steamship, Captain R. Craig, from Glasgow *with passengers* bound for New York on 21 November 1854, also on 19 December 1854, and in 1856.
[EEC#22632/22653][CM#20703]

NIAGARA, Captain Cole, from the Clyde to New York on 6 July 1845, [SG#14/1418]; Captain Munro, from the Clyde to Montreal on 9 May 1850. [EEC#21964]

NICHOLAS BIDDLE, 800 tons, Captain Hiern, from Glasgow to New York on 16 January 1841; from Glasgow *with passengers* to New York on 15 July 1841; Captain Green, from Glasgow *with passengers* bound for New York on 29 July 1844.
[GSP#641/668/673/866]

NICKOLENEEGEE, from the Clyde to Boston in July 1854.
[EEC#22618]

NILE OF DUNDEE, a brig, bound for Quebec in June 1844.
[GSP#866]

NILE, Captain Cromwell, from Ardrossan to New York on 8 March 1849. [EEC#21783]

NIMROD, Captain March, from Aberdeen *with passengers* bound for New York on 30 May 1838. [AJ#4715]

NINA, Captain Bell, from Montrose to Quebec 2 April 1858. [CM#21381]

NITH, Captain Shaw, from Tobermory, Mull, *with 315 passengers from Skye* bound for Prince Edward Island and Cape Breton Island, arrived in Prince Edward Island on 14 September 1840; from Stornaway *with 200 passengers* bound for Cape Breton Island in 1843. [IC,12.8.1840][TGSI.55.344][AJ#4841][TIM#18.34]

NONANTUM, Captain King, from Glasgow *with passengers* bound for Boston in August 1842, [GSP#765]

NORTH AMERICA, 500 tons, Captain Baker, from Glasgow *with passengers* bound for New York on 10 September 1840; from Glasgow to Philadelphia in April 1841; Captain Hall, from Glasgow *with passengers* bound to New York on 22 July 1842. [GSP#659/690/825]

NORTH AMERICAN, 640 tons, Captain Louder, from Glasgow to New York on 19 May 1840; from Glasgow to New York on 7 September 1840; from Glasgow via Londonderry *with passengers* to Portland 15 March 1861. [GSP#673/690][S#1757]

NORTH BRITON, from Glasgow via Londonderry *with passengers* to Portland 22 February 1861. [S#1757]

NORTHUMBERLAND, Captain Mitchell, from Tobermory, Mull, *with 356 passengers, mostly from South Uist* bound for Sydney, Cape Breton Island in Spring 1832, landed at Sydney, Cape Breton Island, on 10 September 1832. [CM#17337][CNSHS#23.46][PANS#282/48]

NORTHUMBERLAND, Captain James McKinlay, from Leith *with passengers* bound for Savannah on 23 November 1840. [EEC#20129]; 377 tons, Captain James, from Glasgow *with passengers* bound for Prince Edward Island in September 1841. [GSP#681]; Captain McKinlay, from the Clyde to Dalhousie on 29 July 1845, [SG#14/1422]; Captain Wyllie, from the Clyde to Quebec on 4 May 1847. [EEC#21497]

NOVA SCOTIAN, Captain Hatfield, from the Clyde to Yarmouth, Nova Scotia, on 27 February 1851, arrived in Boston on 13 April 1851; from Glasgow via Londonderry *with passengers* to Portland 8 February 1861 [EEC#22090/22114][S#1757]

NUBIA, Captain Large, arrived in New Orleans 20 December 1860 from the Clyde. [S#1737]

OBERLIN, 400 tons, Captain J.C.Hott, from Glasgow *with passengers* bound for Boston on 26 June 1844. [GSP#860]

OBERON, 537 tons, Captain Addie, from Glasgow to Quebec in April 1841; from Glasgow *with passengers* bound for Quebec on 2 May 1843. [GSP#657/801]

OCEAN, 500 tons, Captain Willard, from Glasgow to New York on 15 May 1840, [GSP#673]; from Portree, Skye, *with 335 passengers* bound for Prince Edward Island, arrived there on 31 July 1841. [PAPEI] [TIM#18.35]; master George McKenzie, from Portree, Skye, *with 238 passengers* bound for Prince Edward Island in 1848, [[PAPEI:MG24,I.10]; Captain Perkins, from the Clyde to Boston on 21 March 1850. [EEC#21943]

OCTARORA, 540 tons, Captain Smith, from Glasgow to Philadelphia in July 1841. [GSP#668]; 628 tons, from Glasgow to Canada *with 59 passengers* on 26 July 1843, [BPP.35.503]

ODESSA, 488 tons, Captain Vaughan, from Glasgow *with passengers* bound for New York on 24 April 1841; from Glasgow *with passengers* bound for New York on 10 October 1841. [GSP#660/684]

OGLETHORPE, 360 tons, Captain Scott, from Port Glasgow *with 2 passengers* bound to New York on 12 November 1838. [SG#7/718]

OHIO, 1200 tons, Captain Lowber, from Glasgow *with passengers* bound for New York on 13 April 1843. [GSP#799]

OHIO, 768 tons, Captain Lyons or Putnam, from Glasgow *with passengers* bound for New York on 1 July 1844. [GSP#861]; Captain Philips, from the Clyde to New York on 2 May 1850; Captain Conklin, from the Clyde to New York on 13 February 1853. [EEC#21963/22395]

ONDIAKA, 748 tons, Captain Childs, from Glasgow *with passengers* bound for New York on 22 June 1842. [GSP#719]

ONECO, 733 tons, Captain Drew, from Glasgow to Boston in July 1841; from Glasgow to Boston on 13 June 1842. [GSP#668/719]

ONTARIO, a 640 ton American ship, Captain Jamieson, from Glasgow *with passengers* bound for New Orleans on 18 September 1841. [GSP#682/684]

ONTARIO, 460 tons, from Glasgow to Montreal in March 1845. [EEC#21159]

ONYX, Captain Hogg, from Leith to Miramachi in April 1840, [LCL]; from Grangemouth to Miramachi on 3 April 1849; from Dundee to Miramachi on 21 July 1849; arrived in Quebec on 18 May 1850 from the Clyde; from the Clyde to St John, New Brunswick, on 21 March 1850,

[EEC#21793/21840/21978/22099]; from the Clyde **with 6 passengers from Tiree** bound for Miramachi in July 1851. [GHF#326][Argyll Estate Papers#1805, Inveraray Castle][EEC#22148]

OPHELIA AND ANN, Captain Wright, from Stornaway to Quebec on 22 April 1850. [EEC#21960]

ORB, Captain Blake, from Dundee to New York on 30 July 1830. [PA#50]

OREGON, 675 tons, Captain Gledon, from Glasgow to New York on 3 March 1841. [GSP#653]; Captain Crawford, from the Clyde to Quebec and Montreal on 2 September 1850. [EEC#22013]

ORIENT, Captain Smith, from Aberdeen to Cape Breton on 10 May 1849. [EEC#21809]

ORIZEMBO, 660 tons, Captain Marcey, from Glasgow **with passengers** bound for New Orleans on 19 September 1841. [GSP#683]

ORLEANS, 410 tons, from Glasgow to New Orleans on 30 September 1840. [GSP#693]

OROMOCTO, Captain Joslin, from the Clyde to St John, Newfoundland, on 13 July 1850. [EEC#21993]

ORPHEUS, 575 tons, Captain Cole, from Glasgow **with passengers** bound for New York on 25 May 1840; from Glasgow to New York on 25 September 1840. [GSP#676/693]

ORSO, Captain Fowler, from the Clyde to Quebec in April 1858, [CM#21397]; Captain Jones, from Ardrossan to New Orleans on 7 January 1859. [CM#21/623]

OSPREY, 600 tons, master James Salmon, from Greenock **with passengers** bound for New York on 28 May 1831. [PA#91]

OSPREY, 382 tons, from Leith **with passengers** bound for New York on 3 February 1837, [AJ#4643]; from Leith via Caithness **with 115 passengers** bound for Pictou, Nova Scotia, in 1840. [IC,5.8.1840][EC#20041][LCL]

OSWEGO, arrived in New Orleans 31 December 1860 from the Clyde. [S#1741]

OTHELLO, Captain McDonald, from the Clyde to Newfoundland on 26 June 1851, [EEC#221141]

OTTAWA, Captain McArthur, from the Clyde to Montreal on 21 March 1850.[EEC#22099]

OULAKATAN, from the Clyde to Quebec in May 1854. [EEC#22595]

OXFORD, Captain Davidson, from Cromarty **with passengers** to Quebec in June 1832. [CM#17326]

OXFORD, Captain Burns, from Greenock to Miramachi on 25 July 1838; from Port Glasgow to Miramachi on 12 April 1839; from Greenock to Miramachi on 7 August 1839. [SG#7/685; 8/761; 8/793]

OXFORD, 760 tons, Captain Rathbone, from Glasgow to New York on 7 May 1840; from Glasgow *with passengers* bound for New York on 19 August 1840; from Glasgow to New York on 19 April 1841; from Glasgow *with passengers* bound for New York on 19 September 1841; from Glasgow *with passengers* bound for New York on 7 May 1843 and on 7 September 1843. [GSP#660/673/677/685/791]; Captain Burns, from the Clyde to Miramachi on 7 April 1849; from the Clyde to Miramachi on 14 July 1849; from the Clyde to Miramachi on 7 April 1850; from the Clyde to Miramachi on 7 April 1851; from the Clyde to Miramachi on 7 July 1851. [EEC#21795/21837/21951/22105/22144]

PACIFIC OF ABERDEEN, a 386 ton barque, Captain John Morrison, arrived at Quebec 11 June 1836 *with passengers* from Aberdeen; from Aberdeen *with passengers* bound for Miramachi on 10 September 1836; from Aberdeen to Quebec on 3 April 1837; from Aberdeen *with passengers* bound for Quebec on 18 August 1837; from Aberdeen to Restigouche on 6 April 1838; from Aberdeen *with passengers* bound for Miramachi on 8 April 1839; from Aberdeen to Quebec on 21 August 1839; from Aberdeen to Restigouche on 12 April 1840; from Aberdeen to Restigouche in July 1840, arrived in Dalhousie on 7 September 1840 from Aberdeen, [AJ#4619/4626/4650/4674/4709/ 4760/4781/4814/4832/4842]; from Scrabster *with 190 passengers, mostly from Reay* bound for Quebec on 20 April 1841, [IC, 27.4.1841]; arrived in Quebec *with passengers* in 1842. [EEC#20386]; from Wick to Canada *with 39 passengers* on 13 April 1843, from Wick to Canada *with passengers* on 25 April 1844,[BPP.35.503]

PACIFIC, 640 tons, Captain Hale, from Glasgow *with passengers* bound for New York on 21 July 1844. [GSP#866]

PALANDER, Captain Wyman, from the Clyde to New York on 12 May 1850; Captain Lovett, from the Clyde to Boston on 9 November 1850; from the Clyde to Boston on 13 June 1851. [EEC#21967/22042/22135]

PALESTINE, 533 ton barque, Captain Thomas Masters, from Glasgow *with passengers* bound for Boston on 9 February 1849, [SG#18/1788]; from the Clyde to New York on 29 June 1849, [EEC#21831]

PALMYRA, 630 tons, Captain Cushing, from Glasgow *with passengers* bound for Boston on 1 August 1841. [GSP#676]

PANAMA, *with 280 passengers from Scourie, Sutherland* bound for Canada West on 28 May 1847, who settled in Zorra township. [GHF#324][NLS.Sutherland Papers#313/2737]

PANTHEA, 730 tons, Captain Goodmanson, from Glasgow **with passengers** bound for New York on 5 August 1841. [GSP#676]

PARAGON, a brig, from Cromarty **with possibly 100 passengers** bound for Pictou, Nova Scotia, in 1835.

PARKINS, a brig, Captain Younger, arrived in Quebec **with 96 passengers** on 27 July 1834 from Leith and Berwick. [AJ#4522][MG]

PATRICK, Captain Stephen, arrived in Quebec on 18 July 1840 from Fraserburgh. [AJ#4828]

PATRICK HENRY, 1030 tons, Captain Delano, from Glasgow to New York on 25 April 1841. [GSP#661]

PATRIOT, from Aberdeen **with passengers** bound for Canada, wrecked off Gaspe, crew and passengers saved, 1834. [FJ#78]

PATRIOT, Captain Stephen, from Fraserburgh to Quebec on 29 April 1840. [AJ#4817]

PATRIOT, a 261 ton brig, Captain F. Webster, from Leith **with passengers** bound for Montreal on 30 March 1841. [EEC#20172]

PATRIOT, Captain Carning, from the Clyde to Boston on 31 March 1849. [EEC#21858]

PAULINE, Captain Fessenden, from the Clyde to Boston on 10 August 1849. [EEC#21848]

PEACE, Captain Stevenson, from Leith to New York on 29 March 1834. [FJ#66]

PEKIN OF LIVERPOOL 288 ton brig, Captain Blair, from Glasgow on 21 June 1839 via Stornaway **with 266 passengers** bound for Prince Edward Island, arrived there 21 August 1839. [SG#8/780] [PAPEI][TIM#18.33]; Captain Crawford, from the Clyde to Montreal on 10 May 1851, [EEC#22120]

PENNINGHAME, Captain Simm, from the Clyde to Montreal on 16 June 1850. [EEC#21981]

PENNSYLVANIA, 677 tons, Captain Drummond, from Glasgow **with passengers** bound for New York on 19 July 1841. [GSP#673]

PERDONNET, 490 tons, Captain Foote, from Glasgow **with passengers** bound for New Orleans on 10 August 1841. [GSP#676]; from Glasgow to Canada **with 37 passengers** on 10 September 1843, [BPP.35.503]

PERI, from Glasgow to Nova Scotia in September 1855. [EEC#322789]

PERSEVERANCE, from Greenock **with 72 passengers** bound for New York on 22 July 1834. [SG#3/270]; Captain Robinson, from Dundee to St John on 6 June 1848; from the Clyde to Boston on 27 May 1849. [EEC#21668/21816]

PERTHSHIRE OF GLASGOW, 530 tons, Captain Robert Simpson, from Glasgow *with passengers* to New York on 24 May 1842, [GSP#711]; bound for Charleston in April 1843;from the Clyde to Port Wallace, Nova Scotia, on 10 July 1845, [SG#14/1419]; Captain Johnstone, from the Clyde to New York on 11 May 1847; from the Clyde to Pictou on 2 May 1848; from the Clyde to Halifax on 28 March 1849; from the Clyde to Pictou on 26 July 1849; from the Clyde to Pictou, arrived there on 14 May 1850; Captain Tait, from the Clyde to Boston on 27 July 1850; from the Clyde to Pictou on 14 September 1850; *with 437 passengers from Barra and South Uist* bound for Halifax(?),Canada, in 1851. [GHF#326] [EEC#20373/21500/21653/21790/ 21843/21976/21999/22019/22105]

PERU, 460 tons, from Glasgow to Baltimore in May 1841. [GSP#662]

PERUVIAN, Captain Robertson, from the Clyde to St John's on 23 March 1849; from the Clyde to Boston in May 1853. [EEC#21789/22440]

PETREL, a 800 ton steam ship, master R.H.C.Tims, from Glasgow *with passengers* bound for New York on 7 November 1854. [EEC#22633]

PHOENIX, a 700 ton brig, master John Cochrane,from Greenock *with 132 passengers* bound for the Bay of Chaleur, Cape Breton and Prince Edward Island, 28 March 1832, most of them were landed at Pictou in May 1832, [GkAd#3820][TN:17.5.1832]; arrived at Three Rivers, PEI, on 11 May 1832 *with around 35 passengers* from Greenock. [TIM#17.35]; Captain Walker, from Greenock to New Carlisle on 10 April 1839; from Greenock *with 12 passengers* bound to New Carlisle on 18 July 1839. [SG#8/759; 8/788]

PHOENIX, from the Clyde to St John's, New Brunswick, in June 1843. [EEC#20636]; Captain Kerr, from the Clyde to St John, New Brunswick, on 31 July 1845, [SG#14/1424]

PHOENIX, 700 tons, Captain George Sangster, from Greenock *with passengers* bound for New York on 30 May 1844. [GSP#857]

PILGRIM, a 280 ton brig, master George Allan, from Aberdeen to Restigouche and Quebec on 3 May 1837; from Aberdeen to Quebec on 21 June 1838. [AJ#4661/4718/4720]

PILGRIM OF NEW YORK, 378 tons, Captain John E. Williams, from Glasgow *with passengers bound for* New York on 1 July 1848, [SG#17/1731]; from Glasgow to New York on 28 June 1849, [SG#18/1829]; from the Clyde to Baltimore in August 1849; Captain Richardson, from the Clyde to St John, New Brunswick, on 8 October 1850; arrived in Boston on 20 April 1851 from the Clyde. [EEC#21853/22029/22117]

PITT OF AYR, Captain MacKenzie, bound for Quebec in July 1840; from Ayr bound for the Bay of Chaleur in May 1843. [EEC#20086/20612]

PLENDAR, Captain Lovett, from the Clyde to Boston on 15 June 1848. [EEC#21670]

POLLOCK, Captain McIntyre, from the Clyde to Miramachi on 12 April 1851; from the Clyde to Miramachi on 17 July 1851, [EEC#22108/22148]

POLLY, from Portree, Skye, *with passengers* bound for Nova Scotia, wrecked off Prince Edward Island in 1841. [TIM]

POLLY, from the Clyde to Quebec in April 1853. [EEC#22424]

POMONA OF ALLOA, a 359 ton brig, Captain Beveridge, from Leith to Quebec on 9 August 1839; from Alloa to Quebec 1 April 1840; Captain Robert Templeton, from Leith to Miramachi on 2 April 1841; from Leith to Miramachi in August 1843; from Leith to Miramachi on 30 March 1846; from Leith to Miramachi on 2 April 1847; Captain Younger, from Leith to Miramachi on 4 April 1848; from Leith to Miramachi on 27 March 1849, arrived in Miramachi from Leith on 7 May 1849; from Leith *with passengers* bound for Miramachi on 27 March 1850; from Leith *with passengers* bound for Miramachi on 3 August 1850; from Leith to Quebec on 27 March 1851; from Leith to Quebec on 24 March 1853; from Leith to St John, New Brunswick, on 11 August 1853; from Leith to Quebec in May 1854; Captain Cameron, from Leith to Quebec 15 August 1854. [LCL#3453/3870/3974/4182/4222/4277] [EEC#19936/211312/21452/21619/21776/21792/21817/21925/21995/22023/22085/22393/22467/22611]

PORTAFERRY, from Greenock *with 105 passengers* bound for Canada in April 1833. [Times#15146]

PORTIA, a bark, Captain Hurst, from Greenock *with 171 passengers* bound for Quebec, arrived there on 12 August 1834. [MG]

POTOMAC, a 400 ton American ship, Captain Drew, from Glasgow *with passengers* bound for Philadelphia on 1 April 1843. [GSP#796]

PRESIDENT SMIDT, Captain Meyer, from the Clyde to New York on 15 April 1851, [EEC#22109]

PRIMROSE, from Ardrossan to Boston in July 1854. [EEC#22619]

PRINCE ALBERT, a 270 ton brig, from Dundee to Canada *with 17 passengers* on 2 November 1842, [BPP.35.503]; Captain Clerk (or Alexander Rodger), from Leith *with passengers* to Quebec and Montreal on 23 May 1849; Captain Roger, from the Clyde to Boston on 26 February 1851. [EEC#21804/21814/21799/22088]

PRINCE GEORGE OF ALLOA, a 312 ton brig, Captain Thomas
Morrison, from Leith to Quebec on 1 April 1829; from Leith to
Quebec on 7 August 1829; from Leith to Quebec on 17 August
1830; from Leith *with passengers* bound for Quebec on 24
July 1831; from Leith *with 12 passengers* to Quebec in
August 1832, [CM#17342][LCL#2028]; from Leith *with 36
passengers* to Quebec 15 August 1833, [LCL#2136]; Captain
MacFarlane, from Leith *with passengers* bound for Quebec
on 5 August 1839; from Alloa to Quebec on 1 April 1840; from
Leith to Quebec on 29 July 1840; from Leith to Quebec on 8
April 1841;from Alloa to Quebec in June 1842; from Leith
bound for Quebec on 22 July 1843; from Leith to Quebec on 30
July 1841; from Leith *with passengers* bound for Quebec on
22 July 1843; from Leith to Miramachi 20 August 1844; from
Leith to Quebec on 30 March 1846; from Leith to Quebec on 2
April 1847; Captain John Young, from Leith to Quebec on 3
April 1848; from Leith to Quebec on 27 March 1849; from Leith
to Quebec on 1 August 1849; from Leith *with passengers*
bound for St John's, New Brunswick, on 27 March 1850;
Captain Maxwell, from Troon via the Isle of Lewis *with 203
passengers* bound for Quebec on 27 May 1851; from Alloa via
Leith to Quebec in March 1853
[GHF#325][LCL#1/96/1680/1715/1824/2759/3183/3255/3870/
3455/4184/4217/][EEC#18670/19922/20078/20030/20236/
20628/21315/21452/21622/21776 /21792/21844/21925/22130]
[S#24/2141]

PRINCE GEORGE, Captain Ferguson, from Troon to Quebec on 11
April 1848. [EEC#21645]

PRINCE OF WALES, Captain Facy, from the Clyde to St John's, New
Brunswick, on 4 September 1849. [EEC#21859/21868]

PRINCESS, Captain Crosby, from Ardrossan to Boston on 9 August
1849. [EEC#21848]

PRINCESS ROYAL, 338 tons, Captain Whiteney, from Leith to
Quebec on 15 June 1841 [LCL#3474]

PRINCESS VICTORIA, Captain McGawne, from Troon to St John,
New Brunswick, on 24 September 1849; Captain Macbride,
from Ayr to St John, NB, 1 April 1858
[EEC#21872][CM#21381]

PROGRESS, from the Clyde to New York in June 1853, [EEC#22453]

PROVINCIALIST, Captain Williams, from Troon to Philadelphia on
27 March 1849. [EEC#21791]

PRUDENCE, 320 tons, from Glasgow to St John's, New Brunswick, in
April 1841, [GSP#657]

PORTA, a barque, From Lochindal *with passengers* bound for
Quebec in June 1834. [FJ#79]

PROMISE, 446 tons, Captain McKennell, from Glasgow *with passengers* bound for Quebec and Montreal on 1 April 1844. [GSP#848]

PSYCHE, Captain Dishman, from Aberdeen to Boston on 25 March 1837. [AJ#4654]

PURSUIT, a 350 ton brig, Captain Alexander, arrived in New York on 9 June 1834 from Aberdeen, [FJ#79] [AJ#4514]; from Dundee *with passengers* bound for New York on 1 June 1840. *"cabin passengers, including provisions £14, steerage excluding provisions £4"* [EEC#20052] [S#24/2123]; Captain Spence, from Glasgow *with passengers* bound to St John's, New Brunswick, on 25 July 1842.[GSP#826]; Captain Evans, from Glasgow *with passengers* to New York 13 April 1849, [EEC#21798] [SG#18/1805]

QUEBEC, master William Baxter, from Port Glasgow on 1 May 1833 *with 5 passengers from Glasgow* bound for St John, New Brunswick, arrived there on 1 May 1833. [PANB]

QUEBEC, Captain Renton, from the Clyde to Quebec on 11 April 1851, [EEC#22108]; Captain Irvine, from Ardrossan to Quebec 9 April 1858, [CM#21388]

QUEBEC PACKET, a 300 ton brig, arrived in Quebec on 30 April 1827 from Aberdeen. [QueGaz.#3735]; Captain Anderson, from Aberdeen *with 3 passengers* bound to Quebec on 21 July 1834, arrived there on 1 September 1834, [MG]; Captain W. Stephen, from Aberdeen *with passengers* bound for Quebec on 26 August 1836; from Aberdeen on 30 May 1837 *with 31 passengers* bound for Quebec, arrived there 22 July 1837, [AJ#4515/4625/4659] [FAO#117]; from Leith 1 July 1840 via Cromarty on 17 July 1840 *with 117 passengers mostly from Caithness* bound for Quebec and Montreal, arrived in Quebec on 11 September 1840. [S#24/2134][EEC#20068][IC,5,8,1840][AJ#4842]

QUEEN, Captain Evans, from Glasgow to Boston in August 1843. [EEC#20656]

QUEEN OF SHEBA, 550 tons, Captain Francis Caddell, from Leith *with passengers* bound for San Francisco in September 1850. [EEC#22005]

QUEEN POMARE, Captain Wiseman, from the Clyde to St John's, New Brunswick, on 31 March 1849. [EEC#21792]

QUEEN VICTORIA, Captain Rosie, from Aberdeen to Quebec on 24 August 1838; from Aberdeen to Quebec on 18 August 1839. [AJ#4729/4780]; from Aberdeen to Quebec on 10 April 1841; from Aberdeen to Quebec 17 April 1844. [LCL#3250/3456]

QUEEN VICTORIA, 720 tons, Captain Thomson, from Glasgow *with passengers* bound for New York on 13 September 1840.
[GSP#690]

RACHEL, Captain Irvine, from Leith to Quebec on 16 July 1829; from Leith to Quebec and Montreal in July 1832.
[LCL#1710/2019]

RAMBLER, from the Clyde to St Johns, Newfoundland, in April 1860.
[DC#23493]

RAMNAIRE, from the Clyde to St John's, New Brunswick, in August 1843. [EEC#20648]

RANKIN OF GLASGOW, bound for Mobile in March 1844; Captain Lawson, from the Clyde to Quebec on 7 April 1851.
[EEC#21031/22105]

RAVEN, 339 tons, from Glasgow *with passengers* bound for Quebec and Montreal on 15 May 1841. [GSP#662]

REBECCA, Captain Gellatly, from Glasgow *with 10 passengers* bound for Quebec and Montreal on 29 August 1834.
[SG#3/275]

RECTITUDE, Captain Smellie, from Dundee to Quebec 27 July 1854.
[LCL#4323]

RED ROVER, Captain Grant, from Aberdeen to Charleston on 27 August 1836. [AJ#4625]

REGATTA, Captain Ouston, from Leith to Newfoundland in March 1833. [LCL#2090]

REGENT, Captain Steel, from Leith *with 162 passengers* bound for Quebec and Montreal on 1 June 1829. [LCL#1685]

REGULUS, Captain Child, from Greenock bound for New Orleans on 26 January 1844. [GSP#841]

RENFREWSHIRE, 841 tons, from Port Glasgow on 21 April 1842 *with 536 passengers* bound for Quebec, arrived there on 10 June 1842. [EEC#20386] [GSP'714]; Captain McNeil, from the Clyde to Quebec on 5 July 1850; from the Clyde to St John's, New Brunswick, on 26 February 1851; from the Clyde to Quebec on 21 June 1851. [EEC#21990/22088/22138]

RENOWN, a 500 ton barque, from Aberdeen to Quebec in May 1855, [EEC#22749]; Captain William Walker, from Aberdeen *with 2 passengers* bound for St John, New Brunswick, on 23 June 1860. [AJ#5848, 5855]

REPUBLIC, 676 tons, Captain Thompson, from Glasgow to New York on 3 April 1841, [GSP#659]

RESOLUTION, Captain Carter, from Greenock to St John, New Brunswick, on 10 September 1839, [SG#8/803]

RESOLUTION, Captain Hogg, from Peterhead to Quebec on 15 August 1842. [LCL#1/100]

RETREAT, Captain Kinnear, from Leith to Miramachi on 8 April 1829, [LCL#1682]; from Alloa to Miramachi 4 April 1840, [LCL]; Captain Liddle, from Alloa to Miramachi on 27 March 1849; Captain Kerr, from Alloa to Miramachi on 8 July 1850. [EEC#21793/21994]; Captain Hoodlesss, from Alloa to Quebec on 2 April 1851. [LCL#3975]; Captain Young, from Troon to Quebec 22 April 1858, [CM#21398]

RETRENCH, Captain Morrison, from Greenock to New York on 4 April 1839, [SG#8/757]

RETRIEVE, Captain Galloway, from the Clyde to Quebec on 13 June 1849, [EEC#21823]

RETRIEVER, 351 tons, Captain Davidson, from Leith to San Francisco 28 May 1850. [LCL#3887]

REWARD, Captain Hill, from Scrabster to Quebec on 10 April 1848. [EEC#21645]

RHINE, a 235 ton brig, Captain N. Coughlan, from Leith to Halifax in May 1841, [LCL#3466]; from Leith to Halifax and St John's in May 1846; Captain Harward, from the Clyde to Savannah on 19 March 1850. [EEC#21340/22097]

RHODE ISLAND, 370 tons, Captain Baker, from Glasgow *with passengers* bound for New York on 22 July 1841. [GSP#673]

RICHIBUCTO OF ABERDEEN, Captain Ganson, arrived in Quebec on 15 May 1838 from Aberdeen; from Aberdeen to Quebec on 17 April 1847, arrived there on 21 May 1847. [AJ#4718/5180/5189]; from Aberdeen to Quebec on 21 April 1849; from Aberdeen to Quebec on 22 April 1850; from Aberdeen to Quebec on 16 April 1851, arrived there on 26 May 1851; from Aberdeen to Quebec in August 1853; Captain Colvin, from Aberdeen to Quebec on 14 April 1854; from Aberdeen to Quebec in August 1855; from Aberdeen to Quebec 1 May 1858. [CM#21408] [EEC#21801/21955/21997/22110/22475/322789] [AJ#5397][LCL#3875/3979/4292]

RIENZI, 600 tons, from Glasgow *with passengers* bound for New York on 31 July 1840; Captain Smith, from Glasgow *with passengers* bound for Quebec in July 1844. [GSP#685/866]

ROB ROY, 450 tons, Captain March, from Glasgow to Philadelphia on 16 January 1841. [GSP#647]

ROBERT, 310 tons, master John Whitton, from Dundee *with passengers* bound for New York on 27 March 1830. [PA#32]

ROBERT, 318 tons, from Glasgow *with passengers* bound for New York on 31 May 1841. [GSP#662]

ROBERT, a brig, from Greenock *with 51 passengers* bound for Quebec, arrived there in August 1834. [MG]

ROBERT A. LEWIS, from the Clyde to Quebec on 5 July

1851, [EEC#22144]

ROBERT AND MARGARET, from Cromarty *with 66 passengers* bound for Pictou, Nova Scotia, in 1833. [PANS:282/85]

ROBERT ISAAC, 650 tons, Captain Freeman, from Glasgow *with passengers* bound for New York on 5 May 1841; Captain Walker, from Glasgow *with passengers* bound for New York on 21 June 1844. [GSP#662/861]

ROBERT KERR OF GLASGOW, a barque, from Glasgow to New York, sunk at sea on 4 March 1853, *'42 passenger and crew saved by the Douglas, from Newcastle to New York'.* [EEC#22425]

ROBERT MCWILLIAM, 450 tons, Captain Williamson, arrived in Quebec on 3 June 1836 from Aberdeen; from Aberdeen to Quebec on 20 April 1838, arrived there on 17 May 1838; Captain Edwards, from Aberdeen *with passengers* bound for Quebec on 10 April 1839; from Aberdeen *with passengers* bound for Quebec on 11 April 1840; Captain MacDonald, from Aberdeen to Quebec on 13 April 1841, [LCL#3457]; from Aberdeen to Quebec on 18 August 1846, [AJ#4619/4711/4719/4759/ 4814/5147]; Captain McQueen, from Aberdeen to Quebec on 9 April 1848. [EEC#21644]; Captain Webster, from Aberdeen to Quebec on 6 April 1849, [EEC#21795]; from Aberdeen to Quebec on 4 August 1850. [EEC#22003]; Captain Allan, from Aberdeen to Quebec on 19 April 1851, [EEC#22111][AJ#5319]

ROBERT MORRIS, Captain Watson, from Greenock *with 3 passengers* bound for New York on 22 November 1838. [SG#7/720]

ROBERT MORROW, a 282 ton brig, from Leith *with passengers* bound for Montreal on 1 May 1842; Captain Whyte, from Leith to Montreal 5 April 1843 [EEC#20344][LCL#3141]

ROBERTSON, 333 tons, master John Neill, from Greenock *with passengers* to Montreal 17 March 1832, [GkAd#3817] from Greenock *with passengers* bound for Montreal on 24 March 1834; from Greenock *with 38 passengers* bound for Montreal on 28 July 1834, arrived there on 26 August 1834. [MG] [SG#3/227, 270]; Captain Clark, from Glasgow on 9 April 1846, *with 5 passengers* bound for Quebec, arrived there on 21 May 1846, [QG][MT]

ROBIN HOOD, 400 tons, Captain Proctor, from Glasgow to New York on 2 May 1840. [GSP#673]

ROBINA, Captain Martin, arrived in New York 29 December 1860 from the Clyde. [S#1741]

ROCHESTER, 850 tons, Captain Britton, from Glasgow *with passengers* bound for New York on 6 August 1844.[GSP#867]

ROCKALL, a 716 ton American ship, Captain Higgins, from Glasgow *with passengers* bound for New Orleans on 2 October 1842; Captain Evans, from Glasgow *with passengers* bound for New York on 5 August 1844.[GSP#773/867]

ROCKINGHAM, 550 tons, Captain Penhallon, from Glasgow *with passengers* bound for New York on 13 June 1842. [GSP#719]

ROCKSHIRE, 450 tons, Captain Duggan, from Glasgow *with passengers* bound for Quebec and Montreal in August 1842. [GSP#765]

ROGER STEWART OF GREENOCK, 364 tons, master Robert Kerr, from Greenock *with passengers* to New York in April 1830, [GkAd#3435]; from Greenock *with passengers* to New york in March 1831, [GkAd#3627]; master William Gordon, from Greenock *with passengers* bound for New York on 28 April 1838; from Greenock *with 148 passengers* bound for New York on 28 May 1839; [SG#7/654; 8/765, 774]; from Greenock to New York in June 1840, [S#24/2119]; from Greenock *with passengers* bound for New York on 29 April 1842; Captain G. Begg, from Glasgow bound for Quebec in June 1843. [EEC#20633][GSP#710/799]

ROLINA, from Glasgow *with 77 passengers* bound for New York, arrived there on 25 September 1851. [USNA/par]

ROMULUS, a 478 ton barque, Captain Auld, from Greenock *with passengers* to Halifax in March 1830, [GkAd#3432]; from Greenock *with passengers* bound for Halifax, went ashore in the Bay of Islands in April 1831, passengers and crew saved, [AR:30.4.1831]; Captain Banks, from Greenock to Miramachi on 10 April 1839, [SG#8/759]; Captain William Auld, from Greenock *with passengers* bound for St John's, New Brunswick, on 27 July 1840. [GSP#684]; Captain Sangster, from Glasgow *with passengers* bound for New York on 16 June 1848, [SG#17/1724]

ROSCIUS, 1150 tons, from the Clyde to New York on 13 January 1841; Captain Collins, from Glasgow *with passengers* bound for New York on 13 May 1841. [GSP#641/662]

ROSCOE, 600 tons, Captain Gavin, from Leith bound for Miramachi on 23 July 1830, [LCL#1817]; from Leith bound for Miramachi on 28 March 1831. [EEC#18627]; from Leith to Miramachi in August 1832, [LCL#2032]; from Leith *with 14 passengers* to Miramachi 8 August 1835, [LCL#2343]; arrived in Dalhousie in

June 1836 from Leith, [AJ#4619]; Captain Huttleston, from Glasgow to New York on 25 June 1840; from Glasgow to New York on 25 February 1841; from Glasgow *with passengers* bound for New York on 25 June 1842. [GSP#653/680/719]

ROSE, 279 tons, from Aberdeen to Canada *with 94 passengers* on 2 June 1843. [BPP.35.503]

ROSEBANK, 330 tons, Captain Abbott, from Glasgow to Quebec in March 1841;Captain Montgomery, from Glasgow *with passengers* bound for Charlottetown, Prince Edward Island, on 6 April 1843; Captain Thomson, from Glasgow *with passengers* bound for St John, New Brunswick, on 16 March 1844. [GSP#779/796/855/848]

ROSINA, Captain Gale, from the Clyde to Quebec on 10 June 1848; Captain Payne, from the Clyde to Newfoundland on 28 July 1849; from the Clyde to Newfoundland on 10 August 1850; from the Clyde to New York on 3 February 1853. [EEC#21669/21843/22004/22392]

ROTHER, Captain Hall, from Tobermory, Mull, *with 229 passengers from Skye* bound for Cape Breton Island and Prince Edward Island, arrived in Prince Edward Island on 8 September 1840. [TIM#18.34]

ROVER, a brig, Captain Briggs, from Cromarty *with passengers* bound for Pictou in August 1831, *116 Highlanders* arrived in Pictou by late August 1831. [EEC#18689][CP:27.8.1831]

ROWLEY, a brig, Captain Donald MacLarty, from Leith *with passengers* bound for Quebec and Montreal on 9 July 1831. [EEC#18664]

ROYAL ADELAIDE, 416 tons, Captain Stewart or Jamieson?, from Greenock *with 90 passengers* bound to New York on 8 May 1839, [SG#8/755,766, 768]; Captain Potts, from the Clyde to Quebec on 10 May 1847. [EEC#21499]

ROYAL BRIDE, a 300 ton brig, Captain George Welch, from Dundee *with passengers* bound for Quebec and Montreal on 22 June 1842. [FJ#489][LCL#1/83]

ROYALIST, 656 tons, Captain Beveridge, from Leith to Quebec on 27 March 1849; from Leith to Montreal 8 April 1853; from Leith to St John in September 1854; Captain Scott, from Leith to Quebec on 30 June 1855; Captain Mitchell, from Leith to Quebec 2 April 1857; Captain Morris, from Leith to Quebec 13 April 1858; from Leith to Quebec April 1860; from Leith to Quebec on 6 August 1860. [EEC#21790/22758/23525] [LCL#4186/4334/4601/4917/4952][CM#21386]

ROZELLE OF GREENOCK, a schooner, Captain Wilkinson, from Greenock bound for St John, New Brunswick, in August 1844. [GSP#870]

RUNNYMEDE, Captain Prowse, from the Clyde to Newfoundland on 19 July 1851, [EEC#22150]

RUSSIA, a 450 ton American ship, Captain Gilleat, from Glasgow *with passengers* bound for New Orleans in April 1843. [GSP#799]

RUTH ELIZA, Captain Durkee, from the Clyde to Halifax on 5 May 1847. [EEC#21497]

RUTHER, from Aberdeen *with passengers* bound for Halifax in 1847. [CHSNS.23.46]

SAGUNA, Captain Freeman, from the Clyde to New York on 12 June 1851, [EEC#22133]

ST ANDREW, Captain Bruce, from Aberdeen to Richibuchto on 5 August 1837; Captain Paterson, from Aberdeen to Miramachi on 12 April 1839. [AJ#4760/4674]

ST ANDREW OF LIVERPOOL, from Stornaway *with passengers* bound for Sydney, Cape Breton Island, in June 1842. [EEC#20380]

ST ANDREW OF GLASGOW, 499 tons, bound for Quebec in April 1843; from Glasgow to Montreal in March 1845. [EEC#20607/21159]; Captain Wyllie, arrived in Quebec on 9 May 1846 *with 3 passengers* from Glasgow, [MT]; from the Clyde to Montreal on 12 July 1845, [SG#14/1420]

ST CLOUD, 470 tons, Captain Emerson, from Glasgow to New York on 7 July 1841. [GSP#668]

ST FILLAN, Captain Davies, from the Clyde to Newfoundland on 26 July 1845, [SG#14/1422]; from the Clyde to Newfoundland on 13 June 1847; from the Clyde to Newfoundland on 7 December 1850; from the Clyde to Newfoundland on 3 July 1851. [EEC#21514/22054/22142]

ST GEORGE, a steamship, from Glasgow *with passengers* to St John's, Newfoundland, and Charlottetown, Prince Edward Island, on 12 July 1842. [GSP#825]

ST JOHN, Captain Davidson, from the Clyde to Chaleur Bay in August 1837. [CM#18303]; from Greenock to Dalhousie on 10 April 1839; from Glasgow to St John, New Brunswick, on 14 August 1839, [SG#8/759; 8/795]

ST JOHN'S, 450 tons, from Glasgow to St John's, New Brunswick, in July 1842. [GSP#825]; Captain Blyth, from the Clyde to St John, New Brunwick, on 27 February 1853; from the Clyde to Quebec in August 1853. [EEC#22401/22485]

ST LAWRENCE, 400 tons, Captain Chase, from Glasgow to New York on 1 July 1840; Captain Bunker, from Glasgow to New York on 23 March 1841. [GSP#680/657]

ST LAWRENCE, a 510 ton American ship, Captain Hagedome, from Glasgow *with passengers* bound for New York on 10 July 1842. [GSP#724]

ST LAWRENCE, Captain Ferguson, from the Clyde to San Francisco on 1 March 1853. [EEC#22402]

ST LAWRENCE, a 406 ton barque, master James Tulloch, from Aberdeen to Quebec on 14 April 1841; from Aberdeen to Canada *with 139 passengers* on 20 April 1844, [BPP.35.503]; from Aberdeen *with 97 passengers* bound for Quebec on 14 April 1846, arrived there on 20 May 1846, [QG][MT]; from Aberdeen *with passengers* to Quebec in July 1846, in the St Lawrence River on 15 August 1846; from Aberdeen *with passengers (from Aberdeenshire, Orkney and Shetland)* bound for Quebec in April 1847, arrived there in July 1847; from Aberdeen *with passengers* bound for Quebec in August 1847, from Aberdeen to Quebec on 13 April 1848; arrived in Quebec during May 1848 *with 120 passengers* from Aberdeen, [Quebec Morning Chronicle, 17.5.1848]; arrived in Quebec in July 1848 from Aberdeen *with passengers from Aberdeenshire, Orkney and Shetland.;* from Aberdeen to Quebec on 21 April 1849, from Aberdeen to Quebec on 6 August 1849; from Aberdeen to Quebec on 19 April 1850, arrived there on 18 May 1850; from Aberdeen to Quebec on 29 July 1850; from Aberdeen *with passengers* bound for Quebec on 18 April 1851, arrived there in July 1851; from Aberdeen to Quebec on 11 August 1851; from Aberdeen to Quebec in May 1853; arrived in Quebec *with passengers* on 29 May 1854. [LCL#3457/3876/3979] [EEC#21645/21801/21847/ 21958/21978/22000/22110/22448][AJ#5117/5139/5148/ 5172/5193/5377/5389/5397/5405/5553]

ST LEON, Captain Palmer, from Glasgow *with passengers* bound for New York on 7 August 1841. [GSP#676]

ST MARY, Captain Milliken, from the Clyde to New York on 6 August 1849; from the Clyde to Boston on 11 June 1851, [EEC#21846/22133]

SALEM, a 217 ton American ship, Captain C.A.Heirn, from the Broomielaw, Glasgow, *with passengers* bound for New York on 17 February 1844. [GSP#841]

SALUS, Captain Wilson, from the Clyde to Miramachi in July 1837. [CM#18303]

SAMSON, a barque, Captain Murdoch, from Ayr to Quebec on 11 April 1848; from Troon to Quebec on 10 April 1849; from Irvine to Quebec in September 1850; Captain Izat, from Troon to Quebec 16 April 1858. [EEC#21644/21797/22027][CM#21394]

SAMUEL, 558 tons, Captain Fleming, from Glasgow to St John's, New Brunswick, on 12 June 1842. [GSP#719]

SAMUEL CUNARD, Captain Henderson, from the Clyde to New York on 28 June 1851, [EEC#22141]

SAMUEL HICKS, a 1300 ton American ship, from Glasgow *with passengers* bound for New York on 25 March 1843. [GSP#795]

SAPPHIRE, Captain McDonald, from the Clyde to Quebec on 20 May 1851, [EEC#22124]

SARACEN, from Glasgow *with 20 passengers* bound for New York, arrived there on 1 September 1846. [USNA]

SARAH, from Greenock *with 22 passengers* bound for Richibucto in Spring 1832. [CM#173337]

SARAH, a 210 ton brig, Captain Wilson, from Leith *with passengers* bound for St John, New Brunswick, on 27 May 1840. [EEC#20055][S#24/2124]

SARAH, a 350 ton brig, Captain George Allan, from Aberdeen *with passengers* bound for Quebec on 13 August 1839; from Aberdeen *with 36 passengers* bound for Quebec on 2 April 1840; from Aberdeen *with passengers* bound for Quebec on 28 July 1840; Captain Sim, from Aberdeen to Quebec on 7 April 1841 [AJ#4780/4815/4828][LCL#3455]

SARAH, 430 tons, Captain Moon, from Glasgow to New York on 22 February 1841. [GSP#653]

SARAH, 700 tons, Captain McLean, from Glasgow *with passengers* bound for Quebec and Montreal on 5 August 1842. [GSP#826]

SARAH, from Glasgow to Boston in May 1847; Captain Hopkins, from the Clyde to St John's in September 1849. [EEC#21498/21868]

SARAH, Captain Davies, from Aberdeen to St John, New Brunswick, on 10 April 1848. [EEC#21644]

SARAH, Captain Sim, from Aberdeen to Quebec on 8 April 1847, [AJ#5179]; from Aberdeen to Quebec on 23 April 1849; from Aberdeen to Quebec on 11 April 1850; from Peterhead to Quebec on 21 July 1850; from Aberdeen *with passengers* to Quebec on 19 April 1851, arrived there on 28 May 1851. [EEC#21798/21955/21997/22111] [AJ#5389/5397]

SARAH, 536 tons, from Glasgow to Canada *with 58 passengers* on 15 April 1843, [BPP.35.503]; Captain R. C. Tims, from Glasgow on 8 June 1850 *with 225 passengers* bound for New York, arrived there on 18 July 1850; from the Clyde to New York on 12 April 1851. [EEC#21978/22108] [USNA#M237/790]

SARAH, Captain McWhirter, from Leith to Quebec 7 June 1853. [LCL#4203]

SARAH ANN, 377 tons, from Glasgow *with passengers* bound for St John's, New Brunswick, on 6 April 1843. [GSP#779]

SARAH BOTSFORD, a barque, from Glasgow *with passengers* bound for Quebec and Montreal on 17 April 1841. [GSP#660]; Captain McDowall, from Glasgow *with 50 passengers* to Pictou on 2 May 1849; Captain Cameron, from the Clyde to Pictou on 7 April 1851; from the Clyde to Boston on 18 July 1851, [EEC#21805/22105/22150]

SARAH MARKS, 426 tons, Captain Edward Lennox, from Glasgow *with passengers* bound for Boston on 26 July 1842. [GSP#825]

SARA S. of St John, New Brunswick, Captain Suli, from the Clyde to New York sank on 8 May 1853, crew and passengers saved. [EEC#22448]

SARAH WILSON, from the Clyde to New York on 9 May 1848. [EEC#21655]

SARACEN, from Glasgow *with 20 passengers* to New York, arrived there 1 September 1846. [USNA]

SARDIUS, 450 tons, Captain Thayer, from Glasgow *with passengers* bound for New York on 2 May 1840. [GSP#673]

SCIENCE, a barque, master William Snell, from Greenock *with passengers* to New York 15 March 1832. [GkAd#3817]

SCOTIA, 702 tons, Captain Malcolm, from Glasgow to Montreal on 6 June 1839; Captain Jeans, from Greenock to Quebec on 24 August 1839, [SG#8/775; 8/798]; from Loch Eriboll *with 206 passengers from Farr and Tongue, Sutherland* bound for Canada West in May 1848, arrived in Quebec on 7 July 1848. [TGSI#45.340][GHF#324]; Captain Thomas Carey, from Glasgow *with passengers* bound for Quebec and Montreal on 6 June 1849, '*This vessel has eight feet between decks with superior ventilation and is fitted up with every convenience for intermediate and steerage passengers who will be landed free of all head and hospital money. Breadstuffs, water and fuel will be supplied according to the Passenger Act. Tea, coffee, sugar and tobacco may be had on board free. Carries an experienced surgeon.*', [SG#18/1824]; Captain Carey, from Glasgow to Quebec, grounded on Madame Island on 1 August 1849, towed to Quebec. [EEC#21853]

SCOTLAND, a 656 ton American ship, Captain Robinson, from Glasgow to New York on 27 March 1841; Captain Carston, from Glasgow *with passengers* bound for New York on 3 August 1841. [GSP#657/676]

SCOTLAND, a 547 ton American ship, Captain J. Merryman, from Glasgow *with passengers* bound for Boston on 3 August 1844. [GSP#867]

SCOTLAND, Captain Kelso, from the Clyde to Quebec on 28 July 1849, [EEC#21843]

SCOTSMAN, Captain Carmichael, from Leith *with 73 passengers* to New York 25 May 1834. [LCL#2217]

SCOTTISH LASS, from Glasgow to Prince Edward Island, arrived there on 15 September 1853

SEAGULL, Captain Menzies, from Leith to Montreal 13 April 1854. [LCL#4292]

SEA NYMPH, Captain Corbin, from the Clyde to Newfoundland on 24 July 1851, [EEC#22153]

SEDULOUS, Captain Livie, from Aberdeen to Quebec on 16 April 1851, arrived there on 3 June 1851.[EEC#22110] [AJ#5397][LCL#3979]

SEINE, a 280 ton American barque, master L. Walker, from Greenock *with passengers* bound for New York on 7 July 1834. [AJ#4512]

SELMA OF DUNDEE, Captain Taylor, from Dundee to Quebec in March 1846. [DPCA#2333]

SERIUS, 236 tons, *with 117 passengers from Scourie, Sutherland* bound for Canada in 28 May 1847. [GHF#324][NLS. Sutherland Papers#313/2737]

SESOSTRIS, 563 tons, master George McKenzie, from Glasgow *with passengers* 12 January 1842, [GH#4062]; arrived in New York on 25 March 1842 *with 7 passengers* from Glasgow, [USNA.M237/48]; from Glasgow *with passengers* bound for Halifax and Pictou on 17 July 1842; Captain D. Daud, from Glasgow *with passengers* bound for New Orleans on 7 November 1849, [SG#18/1869]; Captain Logan, from the Clyde to Boston on 7 August 1850; from the Clyde to Charleston on 15 December 1850, [EEC#22002/22057]; from Isle of Lewis *with 7 passengers* bound for Canada in 1851. [GHF#325][GSP#724]; from the Clyde to Quebec on 21 June 1851, [EEC#22138]

SEVERN, a 572 ton American ship, Captain Cheever, from Glasgow *with passengers* bound for Boston in October 1842. [GSP#773]

SHAKESPEARE, Captain Rosie, arrived in Quebec *with passengers* on 16 July 1836 from Aberdeen. [AJ#4624]

SHAKESPEARE, 1004 tons, Captain Miner, from the Clyde to New York in June 1840, [EEC#20071]; from Glasgow to New York on 13 April 1841, [GSP#659]

SHANDON, from Glasgow to Quebec in July 1855. [EEC#22770]; Captain Greig, from the Clyde to Montreal 2 April 1858; from the Clyde to Montreal in April 1860. [DC#23550][CM#21381]

SHEFFIELD, 578 tons, Captain Sherry, from Glasgow **with passengers** bound for New York on 21 March 1844.
[GSP#841]
SHELMALARE, Captain Connor, from Greenock to New York on 17 July 1839, [SG#8/787]
SHERIDAN, 1012 tons, Captain De Peyster, from Glasgow to New York on 13 March 1841; from Glasgow **with passengers** to New York on 13 July 1841. [GSP#653/668/673]
SIGNET, Captain Thomson, from Alloa to St John's, New Brunswick, on 26 February 1841; from Dundee to Quebec on 30 June 1849; Captain Mowat, arrived in Quebec on 18 May 1850 from Alloa; Captain McQuat, from Alloa to Quebec on 13 August 1850; from Leith to Quebec 3 April 1851.
[EEC#21781/21832/21978/22008][LCL#3974]
SILAS RICHARDS, 37 tons, from Glasgow to New York on 15 March 1841. [GSP#655]
SILKSWORTH, from Glasgow to Montreal on 2 April 1841.
[GSP#659]
SILLERY, **with 332 passengers from Knoydart** bound for Canada, arrived in Montreal in September 1853.
[TGSI#55.340][GHF#323][PP.46.79]
SIMON, 423 tons, from Glasgow to New Orleans on 20 October 1841, [GSP#684]
SIR CHARLES MCTEAR, from Glasgow to Quebec in July 1850.
[EEC#22007]
SIR CHARLES NAPIER, Captain Tear, from the Clyde to Quebec on 5 July 1850. [EEC#21990]
SIR COLIN CAMPBELL, 900 tons, Captain Pentecost, from Glasgow **with passengers** bound for New Orleans on 1 October 1841; Captain McNab, from the Clyde to Quebec 3 April 1858.
[GSP#683][CM#21382]
SIR GEORGE PREVOST, 400 tons, from Glasgow to Quebec on 13 June 1840. [GSP#678]
SIR HARRY SMITH, Captain Haws, from the Clyde to New York on 3 April 1850; from the Clyde to St John, New Brunswick, on 9 October 1850. [EEC#21900/22029]
SIR HENRY PARNELL, a 209 ton brig, master James Moir, from Dundee to Charleston, South Carolina, on 20 May 1843.
[DW#118]
SIR JAMES, from Glasgow **with passengers** bound for Quebec and Montreal on 15 April 1842. [GSP#712]
SIR WILLIAM MOLESWORTH, Captain Henderson, from the Clyde to New York on 14 February 1851, arrived there on 31 March 1851. [EEC#21084/22108]

SIR WILLIAM WALLACE, a 500 ton brig, Captain Robert Anderson, from Aberdeen *with 39 passengers* bound for Quebec on 24 July 1834, arrived at Grosse Isle on 4 September 1834; from Aberdeen to Quebec on 4 August 1836; from Aberdeen *with passengers* bound for New York on 3 April 1837; Captain Daniel Anderson, from Aberdeen to Quebec on 28 August 1837; arrived in Quebec on 6 October 1837 from Aberdeen; Captain Cumming, from Aberdeen to Quebec on 14 April 1838, arrived there on 9 May 1838; Captain Daniel Anderson, from Aberdeen *with passengers* bound for Quebec on 21 July 1838; Captain Tulloch, from Aberdeen to Quebec on 25 July 1840, arrived in Quebec on 14 September 1840 from Aberdeen; Captain Anderson, from Aberdeen to Quebec 17 April 1844; Captain Jaffrey, from Aberdeen to Quebec on 10 April 1847, arrived there on 25 May 1847; from Aberdeen to Quebec on 23 April 1849; from Arbroath to Quebec on 3 August 1849; from Aberdeen to Quebec on 19 April 1850; from Aberdeen to Quebec on 16 April 1851, arrived there on 26 May 1851; from Aberdeen to Quebec in July 1854; Captain Maurice from Leith to Quebec 17 April 1857.
[LCL#3250/3876/3977/4607]
[EEC#21798/21845/21958/21997/22110/22611]
[AJ#4516/4622/4645/4678/4687/4711/4718/4723/4829/4842/5179/5189/5397]

SIR WILLIAM MOLESWORTH, 468 tons, Captain Laurence, from Glasgow *with passengers* bound for New York on 23 June 1849. [SG#18/1829]

SIR WILLIAM WALLACE, Captain Cunningham, from Scrabster Roads to Quebec 25 April 1858, [CM#21406]

SIRIUS, a steamship, Captain Mowle, from Leith via Cork to New York on 31 May 1838. [LCL#2638]

SIRIUS, a brig, from Wick *with 83 passengers* bound for Pictou, Nova Scotia, in 1847

SISTERS, a 250 ton brig, Captain Michael Beveridge, from Leith *with 30 passengers* bound for Montreal on 25 March 1831.
[EEC#18610]

SISTERS, Captain Miller, from Leith *with 15 passengers* bound for Quebec and Montreal on 2 April 1831. [LCL#1889]

SISTERS OF ABERDEEN, a 280 ton brig, Captain Tulloch, from Aberdeen *with passengers* bound for Quebec on 11 August 1836; from Aberdeen *with passengers* bound for Restigouche on Chaleur Bay, New Brunswick, on 3 April 1837; from Aberdeen to Quebec on 21 April 1838, arrived there on 17 May 1838; from Aberdeen to Chaleur Bay in July 1838; Captain George Hall, from Aberdeen to Quebec in September 1839;

from Aberdeen to Quebec on 25 May 1840,
[AJ#4623/4652/4711/4719/4725/4783/4819]; to Quebec in
July 1840. [EEC#20084]

SISTERS, Captain McKnight, from the Clyde on 30 April to Boston,
[EEC#22115]

SIX SISTERS, a schooner, from Stornaway, landed *100
passengers* from Scotland at Great Bras d'Or in June 1831,
and *20 passengers* were landed at Wallace, Nova Scotia, July
1831. [PANS.Assembly Mss. Misc.B]
[TN:14.7.1831]; from Stornaway *with 102 passengers*
bound for Nova Scotia, landed at Sydney, Cape Breton Island,
on 10 July 1832. [PANS#282/48]

SKEEN, Captain Hunter, from Dundee to Miramachi on 12 April 1830.
[PA#36]; from Leith to New Brunswick on 16 August 1830,
[LCL#1819]

SKEEN, a 400 ton brig, Captain David Bennet, from Leith *with
passengers* bound for Montreal on 1 April 1831.
[EEC#18618]

SOLDAN, Captain Thomas, from the Clyde to Boston on 19 July
1849, [EEC#21838]

SOLWAY, Captain Shandwick, arrived in New York on 14 May 1850
from the Clyde. [EEC#21971]

SOPHIA, a 266 ton brig, master John Neill, from Greenock *with
passengers* to Quebec and Montreal 10 September 1831,
[GkAd#3678]; from Greenock *with passengers* to New York
in January 1832, [GkAd#3706]; master Robert Easton, from
Greenock *with 26 passengers* bound for Quebec in April
1832, [CM#17337] [GkAd#3706/3817]; from the Clyde to St
John, New Brunswick, in June 1840; Captain Paschell, from the
Clyde to St John's, New Brunswick, on 10 March 1850, arrived
there on 25 April 1850; from the Clyde via Sligo, Ireland, to
New York in July 1854. [EEC#20072/21939/21966/22611]

SOPHIA MCKENZIE, Captain McKenzie, from the Clyde to St
Andrews, New Brunswick, on 11 June 1849, [EEC#21822]

SOUTH AMERICA, a 600 ton American ship, from Glasgow to New
York on 19 March 1841; Captain Hagedome, from Glasgow
with passengers bound for New York on 10 July 1842;
Captain Bailey, from Glasgow *with passengers* bound for
New York on 7 March 1843 and on 7 July 1843.
[GSP#655/724/791]

SOUTHPORT, a 500 ton American ship, Captain Hubert, from
Glasgow *with passengers* bound for New York on 25 August
1841. [GSP#679]

SOVEREIGN, 400 tons, Captain Rogers, from Glasgow to Miramachi
on 20 July 1842. [GSP#825]

SOVEREIGN OF SHIELDS, from Dundee to Quebec in July 1854. [EEC#22614]

SPARTAN OF GREENOCK, 796 tons, Captain Durham, from the Clyde to Quebec on 4 August 1849; Captain Muirhead, from the Clyde via Londonderry to Philadelphia on 9 March 1850; to Philadelphia in May 1850; from the Clyde to Quebec on 24 August 1850; Captain George Morrison, from Glasgow *with passengers* to Quebec and Montreal on 10 June 1851; to Quebec in September 1853; Captain Young, from the Clyde to Quebec in May 1858. [CM#21429] [EEC#21846/21939/21976/22010/22492][AJ#5394]

SPEED, a frigate, Captain Grundell, from Greenock *with 316 passengers* bound for New York in May 1850. [EEC#21970]

SPEEDWELL, from the Clyde to Montreal in May 1854. [EEC#22595]

SPRAY, master J. Hume, from Greenock *with passengers* to St John, New Brunswick, in March 1830. [GkAd#3432]

SPRIGHTLY, Captain Johnston, from Dundee *with 60 passengers from Logie Almond, Perthshire,* bound for Quebec on 4 April 1830. [DA, 8.4.1830] [PA#35]

SPRING, Captain Bell, from Stornaway to New York on 9 May 1849. [EEC#21810]

SPRINGFIELD, 547 tons, Captain D. Roy, from Glasgow *with 42 passengers* bound for New York on 17 April 1843. [GSP#799][BPP.35.503]

SPRINGHILL, Captain Auld, from Greenock *with 16 passengers* bound for Quebec on 4 April 1834, [SG#3/234]; Captain Gunn, from Greenock to Quebec on 24 July 1838; Captain Auld, from Port Glasgow to Quebec on 12 April 1839; from Greenock to Quebec on 7 August 1839; from the Clyde to Quebec on 24 April 1849, from Ardrossan to Quebec on 22 August 1849; Captain Elliot, arrived in Quebec on 18 May 1850 from Ardrossan; from Ardrossan to Quebec on 17 August 1850; from Ardrossan to Quebec on 23 April 1851.[SG#7/685; 8/761; 8/793] [EEC#21802/21854/21978/22007/22113]

STAFFA, 268 ton brig, arrived in Prince Edward Island by 12 October 1830 *with passengers* from Greenock; arrived in Prince Edward Island by 17 May 1831 *with 65 passengers* from Greenock; arrived at Three Rivers, Prince Edward Island, by 6 September 1831 *with 156 passengers* from Greenock. [TIM#17.33/34]

STANDARD OF DUNDEE, Captain Roger, from Dundee to New York on 28 January 1830, arrived there on 13 May 1830, [PA#26/42]; *with passengers* bound for New York in June 1832. [CM#17326]

STANDARD, 551 tons, Captain Williams or McMillan, from Glasgow *with passengers* bound for Prince Edward Island on 27 June 1844. [GSP#861]

STATIRA MORSE, Captain Perry, from the Clyde to New York on 4 April 1851. [EEC#22105]

STEPHEN BALDWIN, 630 tons, Captain Gildon, from Glasgow to Philadelphia in 1841. [GSP#653]

STEPHEN WHITBY, 1014 tons, Captain Thomson, from Glasgow to New York on 1 March 1841; from Glasgow to New York on 1 July 1841. [GSP#653/668]

STERLING, 203 tons, Captain Smith, from Dunbar to Miramachi 5 April 1850; from Leith to Montreal in April 1853. [LCL#3872/4185]

STILLMAN, a 333 ton brig, Captain Williams, from Glasgow *with passengers* bound for Pictou and Montreal on 30 June 1841; master Alexander Murray, from Glasgow *with passengers* to Philadelphia on 12 February 1842, *"the railroad now open from Boston to Buffalo renders the route by Boston the most expeditious and cheap mode of travel to Upper Canada, New Brunswick, and the Western States".* [GSP#668/673][GH#4071]; master Alexander Murray, arrived in New York on 11 May 1842 *with over 25 (79?) passengers* from Glasgow. [USNA.M237/48]

STIRLING, a 600 ton barque, Captain Hastie, from Glasgow *with passengers* bound for Quebec on 5 June 1841, [GSP#666]; Captain Robert Cooper, from Dundee *with passengers* bound for New York on 20 March 1842. [FJ#479]; Captain Smith, from Dunbar to Quebec on 12 April 1849. [EEC#21798]

STIRLING CASTLE, a brig, from Greenock on 10 June 1834 *with 363 passengers* bound for Quebec, arrived there via Gross Isle *with 145? passengers* on 9 August 1834. [MG]

STIRLINGSHIRE, 359 tons, from Glasgow *with passengers* bound for Quebec and Montreal on 31 May 1841. [GSP#662]

SUPERB, 630 tons, Captain Stewart, from Dundee to New York in March 1835, [FJ#119];from Dundee to New York in August 1836, [AJ#4624]; Captain Hamilton, from Greenock *with 5 passengers* bound for New York on 12 January 1839, [SG#8/734]; from the Clyde to Baltimore on 28 August 1840, [GSP#689]; Captain John Thomson, from Glasgow *with 220 passengers, mainly farmers from Perthshire, Stirlingshire and Ayrshire* bound for New York in May 1843, [EEC#20612][FJ#540] [BPP.35.503][GSP#799]; from Glasgow *with passengers* bound for New York on 18 May 1844. [GSP#851]; Captain Perry, from the Clyde *with passengers* bound for New York on 6 June 1849, [EEC#21819/21834]

SUPERIOR OF PETERHEAD, a barque, Captain Morrison, from Scrabster, Caithness, *with 194 passengers* bound for Pictou and Quebec in April 1842, [SG.XI.1080]; arrived in Pictou, Nova Scotia, *with passengers* from Scrabster 17 June 1842. [PANS#MG100, vol.167]

SUPERIOR, 600 tons, Captain Allan, from Glasgow *with passengers* bound for New York on 18 June 1844. [GSP#861]

SUSAN, a 390 ton barque, Captain Taylor, from Glasgow *with passengers* to New York on 3 August 1849; from the Clyde to New York on 4 June 1851, [SG#18/1839] [EEC#21845/22130]

SUSAN, a barque, from the Clyde *with passengers* bound for Montreal in June 1851, [EEC#22141]

SUSAN E. SEWELL, 700 tons, Captain Barber, from Glasgow *with passengers* bound for Baltimore on 25 July 1842. [GSP#826]

SUSANNAH, from the Clyde to Providence, Rhode Island, in July 1854. [EEC#22619]

SUSANNAH CUMMING, 545 tons, Captain Salter, from Glasgow to New York on 22 March 1841, [GSP#657]

SUSQUHANNA, 600 tons, from Glasgow to Philadelphia on 8 April 1841, [GSP#659]

SWANTON, 1000 tons, Captain Heath, from Glasgow *with passengers* bound for New Orleans in September 1841. [GSP#677]

SWATARA, 875 tons, Captain Dockendorff, from Glasgow to Philadelphia on 22 March 1841; from Glasgow *with passengers* bound for Philadelphia in September 1841. [GSP#655/676]

SWEET HOME, 340 tons, from Glasgow to Quebec on 20 April 1841, [GSP#659]

SWIFT, Captain Daviege, arrived in Quebec on 27 July 1837 from Cromarty. [AJ#4678]

SWITZERLAND, a 1400 ton U.S Line ship, Captain J. H. Lowell, from Glasgow *with passengers* bound for New York on 29 September 1849. [SG#18/1858]

SYBELLE OF LIVERPOOL. Captain Davison, from Cromarty *with 316 passengers,* wrecked on St Paul's Island on 5 September 1834, all drowned. [FJ#95]

SYLVANUS, a 250 ton brig, from Cromarty *with 196 Highland passengers* bound for Nova Scotia, arrived at Pictou in July 1832. [TN:19.7.1832]; Captain Robert Young, arrived in Dalhousie on 6 June 1836 from Aberdeen; from Aberdeen *with passengers* bound for Quebec on 29 May 1837; from Aberdeen to Restigouche on 9 April 1838; from Arbroath to Quebec in July 1838; from Aberdeen *with passengers* bound

for Restigouche, Bay of Chaleur, on 6 April 1839.
[AJ#4621/4664/4709/4725/4758]

SYLVIA, Captain Hooks, from the Clyde to Dalhousie on 14 April 1849. [EEC#21798]

SYMETRY, 1009 tons, Captain Whitney, from Glasgow *with passengers* bound for New York on 7 May 1841. [GSP#662]

SYMETRY, 334 tons, from Wick *with 128 passengers* on 29 April 1843. [Parliamentary Papers, 1844, 181.xxxv]

SYRIA, Captain Thoms, from the Clyde to New York on 4 September 1849. [EEC#21859]

SYRINX, a barque, Captain Seelye, from Glasgow *with passengers* bound for Boston on 1 May 1844. [GSP#854]

SYROPHENICIAN, Captain Grieves, from the Clyde to Savannah on 1 March 1851. [EEC#22090]

TADMOR, Captain Bowie, arrived in New York from Greenock in 1849. [SG#18/1834]

TALBOT, 600 tons, Captain Stokey, from Glasgow *with passengers* bound for New York on 13 August 1842. [GSP#826]

TAMBERLANE, from Greenock *with 357 Highland passengers* bound for Quebec on 14 July 1831; Captain Henderson, from the Clyde to Savannah on 12 May 1848. [EEC#18672/21657]

TAMENEND, a 478 ton American ship, Captain Edwin Lovett, from Glasgow *with passengers* bound for New Orleans on 1 August 1842. [GSP#826]

TANCRED, a barque, master Phillip Blues, from Leith *with 40 passengers* bound for New York in March 1833. [Times#15137] [CM#17395][LCL#2094]

TAROTINO, 561 tons, Captain Smith, from Glasgow *with passengers* bound for New York on 3 May 1841. [GSP#662]

TAY, a 512 ton barque, Captain Wilson, from Greenock to Dalhousie, New Brunswick, on 21 August 1839, [SG#8/797]; Captain John Langwell, from Greenock *with 193 passengers* bound for New York on 20 June 1840, arrived there on 21 August 1840. [GSP#677][NY Evening Post, 19.8.1840] [USNA#M237/83]; Captain Adams, from the Clyde to Quebec and Montreal on 7 April 1849. [EEC#21795]

TECUMSEH, a 550 ton American ship, Captain Ripley, from Glasgow *with passengers* bound for New Orleans on 22 September 1841. [GSP#682/684]

TEZA, 603 tons, from Glasgow to New York on 1 October 1841. [GSP#683]

THALIA, Captain Patty, from Troon to Boston on 7 October 1849. [EEC#21875]

THAMES, a brig, Captain Bell, from Greenock to Quebec on 30 July 1838; from Greenock to Quebec on 4 August 1839. [SG#7/685;

8/792]; arrived in Quebec on 16 May 1850 from Leith; from Leith to Miramachi on 3 April 1851. [LCL#3889/3974]

THAMES OF ALLOA, a 371 ton brig, from Alloa to Canada **with 1 passenger** on 3 April 1843, [BPP.35.503]; Captain Bell, from Alloa to Quebec on 27 March 1849; from Leith to Quebec in August 1849; from Leith via Alloa to Quebec on 9 August 1850; from Leith to Miramachi on 27 March 1851. [EEC#21793/21859/21997/22008/22085]

THETIS, 160 tons, Captain Cowing, from Glasgow to Quebec on 30 June 1838. [SG#7/672]

THETIS, a 209 ton brig, Captain Barbour, from Leith **with passengers** bound for Bathurst on the Bay of Chaleur, on 6 April 1839. [EEC#19879]

THETIS, Captain Patten, from the Clyde to Boston on 10 July 1851, [EEC#22145]

THISTLE, a brig, arrived in Sydney, Cape Breton Island, **with 66 passengers** from Stornaway in 1837. [PANS#338/72; 252/127]

THISTLE OF GLASGOW, a barque, to California in September 1850. [EEC#22109]

THOMAS, 617 tons, from Glasgow to Philadelphia on 8 October 1841, [GSP#684]

THOMAS FIELDING, Captain Hannah, from the Clyde to New Orleans on 1 February 1853. [EEC#22390]

THOMAS GALSTON, 320 tons, Captain Bulla, from Glasgow **with passengers** bound for Miramachi on 16 March 1844. [GSP#848]

THOMAS P. COPE, 800 tons, Captain Murcken, from Glasgow **with passengers** bound for Philadelphia on 8 August 1844.[GSP#867]

THOMPSON, from the Clyde to Quebec in August 1850. [EEC#22024]

THORNTON, Captain Thomson, from Leith to Quebec on 31 March 1830. [LCL#1819]

THREE BELLS, Captain Campbell from the Clyde to Montreal on 23 June 1850. [EEC#21984]

TIGER, a 630 ton American ship, from Glasgow via Gourock **with passengers** bound for America on 18 May 1840; Captain Hart, from Glasgow **with passengers** bound for New York on 26 April 1842. [GSP#674/710]

TIGRIS, from the Clyde to New York in July 1840. [EEC#20086]

TINTERN, a steamship, Captain Thomson, from the Clyde to San Francisco on 19 October 1850. [EEC#22033]

TONQUIN, Captain Reid, from Troon to Boston 12 June 1858, [CM#21442]

TORONTO, Captain Ballentine, from the Clyde to Montreal and Quebec on 22 June 1849. [EEC#21827]

TRANSIENT, 750 tons, from Glasgow to New York on 7 January 1841. [GSP#641]

TRANSIT, from Glasgow to Newfoundland in July 1854. [EEC#22616]

TRAVELLER, a 300 ton brig, Captain Spalding, from Leith to Richibucto on 3 April 1829, [LCL#1681]; from Leith to Miramachi on 3 April 1830, [LCL#1785]; Captain Wighton, from Kirkcaldy to Montreal on 19 March 1833. [FJ#12]; from Dundee via Aberdeen *with passengers* bound for Quebec in 1834. [AJ#4518]; Captain Lyall, from Leith to Dalhousie on 9 April 1842. [EEC#20334]

TREMONT, a 550 ton American ship, Captain Shaw or Gillespie, from Glasgow *with passengers* bound for New York on 22 June 1842. [GSP#719/723]

TRENTON, 630 tons, from Glasgow to Boston on 15 April 1841, [GSP#659]

TRIAD, from Leith to Quebec in June 1843. [EEC#20636]

TRITON, 405 tons, Captain Alexander MacLean, from Leith *with 64 passengers* bound for Quebec on 18 June 1830, [LCL#1807]; from Leith *with 33 passengers* bound for Quebec on 28 March 1831, [EEC#18594] [LCL#19/1888]; from Leith *with passengers* bound for Quebec on 7 August 1831, [EEC#18679]; from Cromarty *with passengers from Morayshire* bound for Quebec in April 1833. [Times#15146]

TRITON, 300 tons, Captain Luce, from Glasgow *with passengers* bound for Boston in June 1844. [GSP#861]

TROUBADOUR, a 300 ton barque, from Greenock *with passengers* bound for Quebec and Montreal on 25 May 1842, [SG#11/1080]

TRUE BLUE, Captain McNicol, from the Clyde to Montreal on 18 August 1849. [EEC#21853]

TRUSTY, Captain Wyllie, from Leith to Halifax on 7 April 1830. [LCL#1786]

TUSKAR, Captain Bangs, from Greenock to Boston on 17 July 1839, [SG#8/787]; from Lochboisdale *with 496 passengers from Barra and South Uist* bound for Quebec on 7 August 1849. [GHF#325][TGSI#55.342][EEC#21847]

TUSKINA, 50 tons, Captain Spencer, from Glasgow to New York on 22 June 1840. [GSP#680]

TUSKIT, from Glasgow to Boston in June 1854. [EEC#22609]

TWO SISTERS, a brig, from the Clyde *with 30 passengers* to Pictou in 1829.

UNDAUNTED, a 377 ton barque, Captain Kinnear, from Leith *with 6 passengers* bound for Quebec on 20 August 1842.
[EEC#20404][LCL#1/100]

UNDAUNTED OF ARBROATH, a brig, from Greenock to New York in June 1849, [EEC#21834]

UNDAUNTED, Captain Johnston, from Aberdeen to Quebec 8 April 1854. [LCL#4290]

UNICORN, 480 tons, Captain Redman, from Greenock to Boston on 25 July 1838, [SG#7/685]; Captain Meagher, from the Clyde to Newfoundland and Halifax, Nova Scotia, on 23 April 1848; Captain Webber, from the Clyde to New York on 27 June 1850. [EEC#21649/21985]

UNION, a 700 ton United States Line ship, Captain Jacob Hersey, from Glasgow *with passengers* to New York on 15 June 1849. [EEC#21825][SG#18/1828]

UNITED KINGDOM, 1225 tons, Captain W. Meiklereid, from Glasgow *with passengers* bound for Quebec and Montreal on 16 April 1859; from Greenock to portland 21 January 1861; from Glasgow *with passengers* to New York 16 March 1861 [CM#21/652][S#1744/1757]

UNITED STATES, 600 tons, Captain Britten, from Glasgow to New York on 1 April 1841; from Glasgow *with passengers* bound for New York on 1 August 1841; Captain Hamilton, from Glasgow *with passengers* bound for New York on 29 May 1842; Captain Meiklereid, arrived in New York 28 December 1860 from the Clyde; from Glasgow *with passengers* to Portland 10 February 1861 [GSP#657/674/712][S#1737/1757]

UNITY, Captain Lawrence, from the Clyde to Quebec on 25 April 1851, [EEC#22115]

UNIVERSE, a 314 ton barque, Captain George Brock, from Aberdeen to Quebec on 8 April 1837; from Aberdeen *with passengers* bound for Quebec on 15 August 1837; arrived in Quebec on 14 May 1838 from Aberdeen; from Dundee via Aberdeen *with passengers* bound for Quebec in July 1838; from Thurso *with 105 passengers* bound for Pictou in 1841. [AJ#4657/4674/4718/4724]

URANIA, a 300 ton brig, Captain John Younger, from Leven *with passengers* bound for Montreal on 29 March 1831; from Leith *with passengers* bound for Montreal on 9 August 1831; from Leven and Leith *with 65 passengers* bound for Montreal in April 1833, arrived there on 4 June 1833, [LCL#2116]; from Leven *with passengers* bound for Quebec and Montreal on 8 June 1834; from Leven to Quebec in May 1837; from Leith to Montreal on 8 April 1840, [LCL]; from Leith *with passengers* bound for Montreal on 1 April 1840.

[CM#18271][FJ#28/64] [FH#593/599][S#24/2108]
[EEC#18608/18679/20014/20027][Times#15146]
URGENT, Captain Pollock, from Troon via the Isle of Lewis **with 370 passengers** bound for Quebec on 27 May 1851.
[GHF#325][EEC#22130]
UTA, 640 tons, from Glasgow **with passengers** bound for Boston on 1 April 1843. [GSP#795]
VASCO DE GAMA, Captain Miles, from the Clyde to Pictou 7 April 1858. [CM#21385]
VELOCITY, Captain Scott, from the Clyde to Boston on 10 March 1850; from Ardrossan, grounded at Truro on 19 August 1850, arrived in Boston on 28 August 1850; from the Clyde to Yarmouth, Nova Scotia, on 23 April 1851.
[EEC#21939/22021/22113]
VERMONT, Captain Perry, from the Clyde to New York on 21 January 1847. [EEC#21452]
VESPER, from Sutherland **with passengers** bound for Canada (?) in 1850, [PGSI.55.340]; sailed from Scrabster Roads, Thurso, **with 24 passengers from Assynt and north west Sutherland** bound for Quebec on 20 June 1851. [IC, 26.6.1851] [HF#324] [TGSI#45.340] [EEC#22137]
VESTAL, Captain Taylor, from the Clyde to Newfoundland on 24 April 1848. [EEC#21649]
VICTORIA, a 252 ton brig, from Dundee **with 130 passengers** bound for Quebec in 1832. [TSD#63]
VICTORIA, Captain Peters, from Leith **with passengers** bound for Montreal on 6 April 1840 [S#24/2110]
VICTORIA, 320 tons, from Glasgow to St John's, New Brunswick, in April 1841, [GSP#657]
VICTORIA, 716 tons, Captain Mahon, from Glasgow **with passengers** bound for Quebec on 18 June 1844. [GSP#861]
VICTORIA, a 251 ton brig, Captain George Peters, from Leith **with passengers** bound for Montreal on 1 April 1840.
[EEC#20014][LCL]
VICTORY, 590 tons, Captain White, from Glasgow **with passengers** bound for Quebec on 8 August 1844.[GSP#867]
VIEWFORTH, Captain Elder, arrived in Quebec on 16 July 1836 from Cromarty. [AJ#4624]
VILLE DE PARIS, 1030 tons, from Glasgow **with passengers** bound for New Orleans on 18 March 1843. [GSP#795]
VIRGINIA, 284 tons, Captain Sinclair, from Glasgow to New York on 30 June 1838. [SG#7/672]
VIRGINIA, 950 tons, Captain Eaton, from Glasgow **with**

passengers bound for New York on 23 April 1843. [GSP#800]

VIRGINIAN, 850 tons, from Glasgow to New York on 1
January 1841 and on 1 May 1841. [GSP#644/661]

VOLANT, Captain Torney, arrived in Norfolk on 22 December 1860
from troon. [S#1737]

VOYAGER, Captain Skeoch, from Leith to Quebec 2 August
1839. [LCL#2759]

VULCAN, Captain Caird, from the Clyde to New York on 4
February 1853. [EEC#22392]

WALES, 447 tons, Captain Watt, from Glasgow to New York 3 May
1840; from Glasgow to New York on 29 June   1841.
[GSP#668/673]

WALLACE, a brig, from Fraserburgh *with 96 passengers* bound
for Quebec on 21 June 1854. [AJ,28.6.1854]

WALLACE, 864 tons, Captain Wilkie, from Greenock *with
passengers* bound for Quebec and Montreal on 23 June 1854.
[EEC#22595]

WALLINGTON, a brig, Captain John Young, from Leith *with 63
passengers* bound for Montreal on 31 March 1831.
[EEC#18604][LCL#19/1888]; from Leith *with 130
passengers* bound for Quebec and Montreal on 1 April 1832,
wrecked on 15 May 1832, *1 passenger drowned.*
[CM#17311]

WALPOLE, a 550 ton American ship, Captain Thomas, from Glasgow
with passengers bound for Boston on 28 June 1842.
[GSP#723]

WANDERER, a 280 ton brig, master Francis Cowan, arrived in New
York on 26 February 1842 *with 6 passengers* from Glasgow.
[USNA.M237/48]

WANDERER, Captain Benson, from the Clyde to Providence on 1
March 1853, [EEC#22402]

WANDERER OF LEITH, Captain Allan, from Alloa to St John's, New
Brunswick, and Quebec in August 1849; Captain Kerr, from
Alloa to St John's, New Brunswick, on 1 March 1850; from Leith
to St John, New Brunswick, in September 1850; Captain
Buchanan, from Leith to Quebec on 25 July 1860. [DC#23522]
[EEC#21835/21856/21937/22029][LCL#4948]

WANDSWORTH, 825 tons, Captain James Sangster, from Glasgow
with passengers bound for New York on 6 June 1842.
[EEC#20381][GSP#715]; Captain Dunlop, from Greenock to
Quebec on 31 July 1845, [SG#14/1424]; from the Clyde to
Quebec on 14 June 1850, arrived at Sydney, Cape Breton
Island, on 20 July 1850; from the Clyde to Quebec in August
1860. [EEC#21981/22007/23532][NAS.RH1.2.783]

WARNER, Captain Croker, from Ardrossan to Newfoundland on 21 April 1849. [EEC#21802]

WARREN, a 900 ton United States Line ship, Captain Job G. Lawton, from the Clyde to New York on 3 March 1849; from Glasgow *with passengers* to New York on 24 June 1849; from the Clyde to New York on 13 April 1850; from the Clyde to New York on 27 July 1850; Captain Lambert, from the Clyde to New York on 7 December 1850, arrived there on 26 March 1851. [SG#18/1828] [EEC#21778/21827/21954/21999/22054/22108]

WARRINGTON, from Kirkcudbright *with farm laborers* bound for America in June 1843. [DS, 14.6.1843]

WARRIOR, Captain Howie, from the Clyde to Miramachi in April 1840. [EEC#20045]

WARSAW, a 600 ton American ship, Captain N. T. Hawkins, from Glasgow *with 9 passengers* bound for New York on 15 June 1845, arrived there on 1 August 1845. [IC,28.5.1845][USNA]; Captain Bruce, from Glasgow *with passengers* bound for New York on 11 July 1841. [GSP#673]

WASHINGTON, Captain McLay, from Uig, Skye, *with 551 passengers* bound for Prince Edward Island, arrived there on 11 August 1841, [PAPEI][TIM#18.35]

WASHINGTON, 1000 tons, Captain Benson, from Glasgow *with passengers* bound for New York on 17 April 1843. [GSP#800]

WATER HEN, Captain Dodds, from the Clyde to Quebec on 16 August 1849, [EEC#21850]; *with passengers from North Uist*, arrived in Quebec in 1849. [GHF#325]

WATERMILLOCK, a 217 ton snow, Captain James Connor, from Glasgow *with passengers* bound for Montreal on 20 June 1844. [GSP#860]

WATER WITCH, Captain Caithness, from Aberdeen to Cape Breton Island on 9 July 1834. [AJ#4514]

WELLINGTON, Captain Forster, from Glasgow *with passengers* bound for Boston on 8 April 1842. [GSP#710]

WESTCHESTER, 700 tons, from Glasgow *with passengers* bound for New York on 28 July 1840; Captain Ferris, from Glasgow to New York on 3 April 1841; from Glasgow *with passengers* bound for New York on 26 July 1842. [GSP#657/685/824]

WEST LOTHIAN, 143 tons, Captain Bell, from Leith *with 21 passengers* bound for Quebec and Montreal in May 1845. [LCL#3361]

WESTMORELAND, Captain Pearson, from Dundee to New York on 13 June 1830; from Dundee to New York on 12 December 1830. [PA#45/72]

WESTMORELAND, a 265 ton sailing brig, Captain Duncan, from Leith *with passengers* bound for Quebec and Montreal on 26

May 1840; Captain Walker, from Leith bound for St John in
May 1843. [EEC#20042/20599][S#24/2117] [LCL#3148]

WESTMORELAND, 400 tons, to St John's on 20 April 1843.
[GSP#800]

WEYBOSSET, a 500 ton American barque, Captain Wescott Harris,
from Glasgow *with passengers* bound for New York on 27
July 1844. [GSP#865]

WILHELMINA, a 400 ton barque, Captain Alexander Hutton, from
Glasgow *with passengers* bound for New York on 10 May
1844. [GSP#853]; Captain Leslie, from Aberdeen to Quebec on
10 April 1848; from Aberdeen to Quebec on 12 April 1849;
from Aberdeen to Quebec on 11 April 1850.
[EEC#21644/21797/21955]

WILLIAM, a 257 ton brig, Captain Harrison, from Leith *with
passengers* to Quebec and Montreal on 25 May 1840.
[EEC#20030/20039]

WILLIAM, Captain Gellatly, from the Clyde to San Francisco on 29
October 1850. [EEC#22037]

WILLIAM BROMHAM, Captain Bromham, from the Clyde to Quebec
on 9 May 1851. [EEC#22119]

WILLIAM BROWN, 540 tons, Captain Thayer, from Glasgow to
Philadelphia on 15 March 1841. [GSP#653/655]

WILLIAM DAWSON, 481 tons, Captain Beveridge, from Alloa to
Quebec 31 March 1840, [LCL#2828]; from Alloa to Quebec in
June 1842, [LCL#1/96]; from Alloa on 2 August 1845 *with 4
passengers* bound for Quebec, arrived there on 8 September
1845. [FAO#79]; Captain Whyte, from Alloa to St John's, New
Brunswick, on 1 March 1849; Captain Hoodless, from Alloa to
St John's, New Brunswick, on 5 March 1850; from Alloa to
Quebec on 30 July 1850; Captain Beveridge, from Alloa to
Quebec 2 April 1851; from Leith to St John, New Brunswick, 15
August 1854; Captain Ness, from Leith to Quebec 10 April
1857. [EEC#21781/21937/22002][LCL#3975/4327/4603]

WILLIAM HENRY OF SUNDERLAND, a brig, Captain Copple, from
Cromarty via Thurso *with 95 passengers* bound for Quebec
in June 1834, arrived there on 14 August 1834,
[AJ#4511][MG]; arrived in Pictou, Nova Scotia, on 28 July 1834
with 102 passengers from Cromarty. [PANS#282/118]

WILLIAM HERDMAN, Captain Manning, from the Clyde to Quebec
on 20 June 1849, [EEC#21826]

WILLIAM HITCHCOCK, a 700 ton American ship, captain Rollins,
from Glasgow *with passengers* bound for New York on 18
July 1849. [SG#18/1833]

WILLIAM HUTT, a 285 ton brig, Captain William Rankine, from Glasgow **with passengers** bound for Quebec and Montreal on 30 May 1851, arrived there on 20 July 1844. [GSP#857/870]

WITCH, from Stornaway to Miramachi on 16 June 1849, [EEC#21827]

WOLFSCOVE OF GLASGOW, Captain Hamilton, from the Clyde to Quebec in June 1832, [CM#17326]; from the Clyde to Quebec, arrived there on 29 May 1833, [SG#2/152]; from the Clyde to Quebec in April 1840, [EEC#20045]; from Glasgow bound for Quebec in April 1843; Captain Farquharson, to St John's, New Brunswick, in May 1849; Captain Cumming, from the Clyde to Quebec on 5 July 1851; Captain Livingstone, from the Clyde to Quebec 9 April 1858. [EEC#20601/21819/22144][CM#21386]

WOLFVILLE, Captain McMillan, from Ardrossan to New York on 24 February 1850, [EEC#21934]; from the Clyde via the Isle of Lewis **with 69 passengers** bound for Quebec on 29 May 1851. [GHF#325][EEC#22127]

W. OUGHTRED, Captain Stephen, from Aberdeen to Quebec on 16 August 1850. [EEC#22007]

XYZ, 450 tons, from Leith **with passengers** bound for Quebec and Montreal on 25 May 1833. [FJ#18]

ZEALOUS, Captain Reid, from Leith **with 137 passengers** bound for Quebec and Montreal on 30 May 1831. [LCL#1905]

ZEALOUS, 350 tons, Captain Bell, from Leith **with 137 passengers** bound for Quebec and Montreal on 1 June 1831. [EEC#18645][LCL#19/1905]

ZENOBIA, 630 tons, from Glasgow to New York on 22 August 1840. [GSP#689]

ZEPHYR, a brig, from Inverness **125 passengers** for Quebec and 51 for Pictou in 1833 [CP:30.7.1833]

ZERO, Captain Harrington, from the Clyde bound for New York, wrecked at Archeveque, Cape Breton, on 18 July 1853. [EEC#22484]

References

AJ	=	Aberdeen Journal, series
ANY	=	Biographical Register of the St Andrew's Society of New York
BB	=	The Book of Barra, J.L.Campbell [London 1936]
BPP	=	British Parliamentary Papers, series
CM	=	Caledonian Mercury, series
CNSHS	=	Collections of the Nova Scotia Historical Society, series
DA	=	Dundee Advertiser, series
DC	=	Dumfries Courier, series
DPCA	=	Dundee, Perth, and Cupar Advertiser, series
DS	=	Dumfries Standard, series
DW	=	Dundee Warder, series
EC	=	Edinburgh Courant, series
EEC	=	Edinburgh Evening Courant, series
FAO	=	From Aberdeen to Ottawa in 1845, G.A.Mackenzie, [Aberdeen, 1990]
FH	=	Fife Herald, series
FJ	=	Fife Journal, series
GH	=	Glasgow Herald, series
GkAd	=	Greenock Advertiser, series
GSP	=	Glasgow Saturday Post, series
IA	=	Inverness Advertiser, series
IC	=	Inverness Courier, series
IJ	=	Inverness Journal, series
LCL	=	Leith Commercial Lists, series
MG	=	Montreal Gazette, series
MT	=	Montreal Transcript, series
NAS	=	National Archives of Scotland
NLS	=	National Library of Scotland
NW	=	Northern Warder, series
PA	=	Perthshire Advertiser, series
PANB	=	Public Archives of New Brunswick
PANS	=	Public Archives of Nova Scotia
PAPEI	=	Public Archives of Prince Edward Island
PB	=	The Pictou Book, G.MacLaren [New Glasgow, N.S., 1954]
PC	=	Perthshire Courier, series
QG	=	Quebec Gazette, series
S	=	Scotsman, series
SCGaz	=	South Carolina Gazette, series
SG	=	Scottish Guardian, series

SHIPS FROM SCOTLAND TO NORTH AMERICA, 1830-1860

ScotGen		Scottish Genealogist, series
SM	=	Scots Magazine, series
TGSI	=	Transcations of the Gaelic Society of Inverness, series
TIM	=	The Island Magazine, series
TN	=	The Novascotian, series
USNA	=	United States National Archives